ENTERING THE STONE

Entering
the Stone

On Caves and Feeling
through the Dark

BARBARA HURD

THE UNIVERSITY OF GEORGIA PRESS
Athens

Published in 2008 by
The University of Georgia Press
Athens, Georgia 30602

Designed by Melissa Lofty
Printed and bound by Thomson-Shore

The paper in this book meets the guidelines for permanence
and durability of the Committee on Production Guidelines
for Book Longevity of the Council on Library Resources.

Printed in the United States of America
12   11   10   09   08   P   5   4   3   2   1

Library of Congress Cataloging-in-Publication Data

Hurd, Barbara.
Entering the stone : on caves and feeling through the dark /
Barbara Hurd.
    p.   cm.
Originally published: Boston : Houghton Mifflin, 2003.
ISBN-13: 978-0-8203-3153-9 (pbk. : alk. paper)
ISBN-10: 0-8203-3153-8 (pbk. : alk. paper)
1. Caving. 2. Caves. I. Title.
GV200.62.H87 2008
796.52'5—dc22   2007044844

*For their continued protection, the actual names and
locations of the wild caves mentioned in this book have
not been disclosed.*

The author is grateful for permission to quote from the
following works: *The Collected Poems of Wallace Stevens,*
© 1954 by Wallace Stevens and renewed 1982 by Holly
Stevens. Used by permission of Alfred A. Knopf, a division
of Random House, Inc. *Selected Poems of Rainer Maria
Rilke: A Translation from the German and Commentary
by Robert Bly,* © 1981 by Robert Bly. Used by permission of
HarperCollins.

An earlier version of "In the Hollow That Remains"
appeared in *Graywolf 5 Forum.*

Entering the Stone was originally published in 2003 by
Houghton Mifflin.

Always carry three sources of light.

— *A Guide to Responsible Caving,*
NATIONAL SPELEOLOGICAL SOCIETY, INC.

Go without sight,
And find that the dark, too, blooms and sings.

— WENDELL BERRY

CONTENTS

ACKNOWLEDGMENTS

Grateful and affectionate acknowledgment, as always, to the Thursday night writing group—Susan Allen, Brad Barkley, Jack DuBose, Mary Edgerly, Michael Hughes, Keith Schlegel, Maggie Smith, and Karen Zealand—and to those who guided me underground and otherwise: Liz, Rich, Amy, Emily, Mike, Debbie, Sue, Kathy, Jenny, J'amie, Jim, Lysa, and Kelly.

Thanks to my agent, Cynthia Cannell, for her hard work and optimism; to Deanne Urmy, the editor every writer dreams of; and to my husband, Stephen Dunn, whose passion and insights have enlivened this work and everything else.

Thanks also to the Frostburg State University for its continued support, to the Elkins Foundation for the gift of time, to Yaddo and The MacDowell Colony, where much of this book was written, and to the National Endowment for the Arts for a Creative Writing Fellowship.

ENTERING THE STONE

1

THE SQUEEZE

I am such a long way in I see no way through,
and no space: everything is close to my face,
and everything close to my face is stone.

— RAINER MARIA RILKE

I'M CLUMSY in a cave. And nervous. My first attempt at caving ten years ago began in inspiration and ended in terror. I'd been teaching creative writing at an environmental camp for middle school students who were scheduled to take a field trip to a nearby cave. For two days before the trip, I primed them with stories about Mohammed in the cave, Plato's cave, why caves so often symbolize rebirth. It's a hidden space, I told them, an unexpected, inscrutable space. Strange things live in there—eyeless salamanders, albino fish, a prophet's epiphanies. I debated whether to suggest to them that going into a cave might be like going inside one's own mind, crawling around in the pitch-black, nook-and-crannied labyrinth of the human psyche. I didn't anticipate trouble. I didn't mention claustrophobia or the guide's warning

1

that we'd need to belly-squirm down the initial passage. We all loved outdoor adventure, and on the day of the expedition, two guides, eleven students, and I fastened the chin straps of our helmets in anticipation and climbed down a rope ladder into a muddy pit, at the bottom of which was the mouth of the cave.

The pit itself was ten feet across, maybe ten feet deep. You could stand in it and look up at the trees arching over it, see the sky, the tops of the high grass that edged it, a sprinkling of field daisies. One guide explained the sloping first passage, how to get through it, what lay beyond. Head first, he said, and then scooch with your elbows. At the far end, he explained, the tunnel opens up on a ledge and then you squirm down into a big room where you can stand and stretch. It was all reassuring, the directions as ordinary as ones you'd give to someone looking for a phone booth.

The trouble started as soon as I bent down and peered into the chute's entrance. It was, by any caver's standards, an extremely easy passage, fairly round, maybe two feet high. It actually looked tidy, a railroad tunnel in some miniature train layout. The first seven feet were lit by daylight that thinned into a smoke-gray, lead-gray charcoal of darker and then dark. I stood up and watched as the kids kept disappearing down it. They'd lean over, stick their faces in, then lie down and start squirming. The last I'd see of them was their feet wiggling, the toes of their boots shoving against the hole's interior floor, and then nothing. My heart started to pound. "Ready?" the last guide asked me. We were the only ones left in the pit. I was supposed to go, and then he'd bring up the rear. "Yep," I said. And stood there. "You okay?" he asked. "Yep," I replied and got down on my hands and knees, down on my elbows, and looked in again. My headlamp threw a small circle of light into what no longer looked tidy, looked, in fact, like something gouged open, the interior walls jutted and slimy. The guide waited. I lowered my upper body and then my hips to the cave floor and dragged myself forward on my elbows, pushing with my right hip and then left, right boot and then left, the tunnel growing darker and muddier, my light smaller and smaller. And then something was moving toward me, not stone, not anything I could see, maybe sound, maybe wind, and then something else: the Mack truck that barreled into my cousin's car moments before his death. I felt it as clearly as if I'd been in that silent car with him, windows rolled up, both of us speechless as an impossibly large pair of headlights, steel bumper, and grille loomed into the side-view mirror, bore down on our watery bodies of burnable flesh. Only I wasn't there, I was here in a dark tunnel and couldn't see what I felt, knew only that I was about to be flattened by the thing that moves inside stone, the thing that was hurtling up that tiny tunnel toward me, who was by now scratching and clawing my way backwards.

When I came back toward him, rear-first, knees bumping in reverse, frantic, I heard the guide scramble out of my way and felt him catch my shoulder as I turned to scurry up the rope and out of the pit. "Just wait for a few minutes," he said. "It'll pass. You can try again. Lots of people just need a few minutes." I looked at him steadily. My voice was eerily calm. "No," I said, one foot on the first rung. "Absolutely not." There was no talking to me, no reasoning at all. Something had been suddenly siphoned out of my mind and all that remained was what I knew not to do, not to try again, not to even look back at. He urged again but I shook him off and climbed out of the pit and into the sunshine.

Claustrophobia? Maybe, though as a child I'd loved hiding in closets, under beds, under attic eaves, inside the three-by-three-foot toy box my father had made out of plywood and painted red. Hallucinations? Maybe. For years, I had no explanation of my cave terror and still don't.

But slowly I did try again. Something drew me, some curiosity about that unexpected terror and a lifelong love of stones. As children, my friend Jeanne and I had created endless small-stone dramas in the woods behind my house, built hospitals for injured stones, performed surgery on them, nursed them back to health. We'd gone on to college together, signed up for two semesters of geology, mostly because we'd heard that in the labs you got credit for rubbing and licking stones. We loved geodes and the rock exposed when road-building crews dynamited away the side of a mountain, anything that let us look at what's been concealed for thousands of years. How could I let one afternoon of terror keep me from the ultimate intimacy with stone: to go inside it? I wanted to try caving again, and so I started in a commercial cave—Howe Cavern near Albany, New York, where more than thirteen million people have gone underground. Surely I could do it too.

Commercial caves—or show caves, as they're often called—are owned by enterprising private citizens or by state and local governments hoping to educate the public and protect a natural resource. Tourist-pleasing spectacles, their interiors are sidewalked and brightly lit, spangled with dripping stalactites highlighted by colored spotlights and sometimes accompanied by piped-in music, all of it so fabulous you can almost forget you're inside a mountain. Anyone capable of a half-mile walk can buy a ticket and go with other visitors and a well-informed guide. Handrails line the walks that wind around formations and up and down the inclines and declines so gently you could probably roller-skate on them. There's no physical challenge and no discomfort a sweater can't solve. In fact, the only danger inherent in such caves is the possibility of thinking that visiting one is the same as caving in a wild one.

Wild caves are not developed in any way. No sidewalks or labeled formations, no blasted-out ceilings to prevent head-bumping, no electric lights or professional guides. Just the dark cave as it formed over millions of years and rarely any public notice about its location. My search for one with an easy entrance began in my hometown bookstore. I bypassed the books of "regional interest" and went right to the owner, whose connections to all things local were legendary. "Sure," he said. "Not that I personally know where the caves are, but I know who does." A few phone calls later and I was talking with a caver in the next town who had a lot of questions about my experience and motivation and a lot of hesitation about taking me underground. Could I rappel? Use a mechanical ascender? Rig a rope someone could trust with her life? "No," I answered, and "no" and "no." But I was reasonably fit and very determined. A month passed and we finally met one morning in a parking lot where she taught me to work the battery-powered headlamp on the helmet she loaned me. And then she went on to give me explicit instructions on wild cave survival—reminders always to go with three sources of light (battery, backup battery, candles, glowsticks), extra water, and an experienced companion. And on cave etiquette—no touching stalactites, no littering. "Yes," I said, "I have them," and "No, I would never." And then we got in her truck and took the back road to a wild cave in West Virginia where four others were waiting for us.

It's April, season of tender green and cows out in the meadows at last after a winter in the barn. I've explained to the two leaders what I want: to crawl around in the dark, to try another tight spot, to be helped through any panic that might follow. I wasn't an idiot anymore about my fear; it wouldn't sneak up on me unexpectedly, leave me a backward-crawling, blathering half-wit. The entrance to this cave is in a cliff on the other side of a stream that divides a meadow. Walking across the new green grass, I look up at the mountain, and though I can't see the opening itself, I can see where the stone gets more convoluted, the folds and crevices deeper, the shadows more suggestive. We scramble up a bouldery slope, inch sideways across a ledge, and suddenly there's the entrance, a rather wide entrance, maybe four feet high. *Easy,* I think. Three of the others go in immediately. Debbie, Kathy, and I sit outside a while. They describe the passage, how it narrows a bit fairly soon but not for long, and ask me how I want to do it. Do I want them in front or behind me? How close? Someone else nearby?

It's an odd experience, being calmly asked how you want to get through a fear that might be about to squeeze you breathless. I think of friends who've helped one another through difficult times. What is it we can offer each other? An unruffled presence, maybe a map of good handholds, words of encouragement. But mostly, perhaps, the obvious demonstration that someone else has been through this and lived. In the middle of a divorce, you want someone nearby who's done it before, who can describe the landscape ahead, who can prove that divorce isn't fatal. When your dog dies, nobody's better than the friend with the most recent dog death in the family. And now, when Jeanne, my childhood friend and stone-loving compatriot, is slowly dying, I want Ann, who survived her sister's death. "Here," your friend says, "put your hand here, your knee over there, find your body's sense of balance, now push with your foot." You know you're in unfamiliar territory, a landscape where you could get lost, wander or grieve forever. You need, more than anything, the willingness to be instructed, and finally you get through it. I want Debbie in front of me, I tell her, close enough so I can touch the heel of her boot. And Kathy behind me, three feet back, her light aimed as far ahead as possible. "Fine," they both say, and we head in. I'm amazed how easy it is to tell them what I need.

We squat and duck-walk a short while and then have to get on our hands and knees. Daylight from the entrance fades. The darkness is broken only by the small lights on our helmets. Debbie and Kathy banter a bit as we crawl, as if we were all sitting around someone's kitchen table. It soothes me, though I keep reaching out my hand, making sure I can touch Debbie's boot. We keep our heads low. The walls aren't muddy here but close enough that if I turned my elbows out as I crawled, they'd scrape against stone. I keep my eyes fixed on Debbie's boots. She doesn't have to push with her feet here and so the boots simply follow her knees, one after the other in a steady pistonlike action I find comforting. I adjust my pace to match hers. When her right knee moves forward, mine does too. Same with the left. First one, then the other. I don't look at anything else. I study the soles of her boots, feel our movements synchronized, as if we're hooked to the same pulley system, ratcheting ourselves forward together in the darkness until I begin to relax a bit, comforted by our steady movement, and am able to swing my head to the side for a second and look at the small circle of the tunnel wall lit up by my headlamp. It's fairly dry, pebbly almost, gray-brown and pocked. And irregular, as if a drunken plasterer had crawled in and slathered mud that then dried in a haphazard pattern of chunks and swipes and small ridges. I'd forgotten how hard stone is, the bony patella of my knees scraping directly on it. Sound is harsh here, too, unmuffled, our boots grating, pants crinkling, water bottles sloshing in the otherwise great silence of a cave. And then the others' voices and the ceiling suddenly rise and I look up. Though it's pitch-black except for our six small lights, I can tell this room is fairly large, twenty by twenty, perhaps, high ceilings and sloping floor. The others have been poking around, waiting for us, eager to move on. Debbie dallies a bit, shines her light into a small den packed with leaf litter, guesses it's a rat who lives in there. Kathy's behind me, searching in her pack for a battery to replace the one that failed partway through the tunnel. Whether it was foolish of her or not, I silently praise her ability to have crawled through by our light, her considerate sense not to announce halfway through that her own had failed. I want to hug everyone, to toast my own feat. I lean against a wall and look at what I've just crawled through. I don't know what's ahead. I do know that's the only way out.

What's immediately in front of us is a fairly smooth passage, an easy walk. I shine my headlamp on the irregular walls, the sloping ceiling. I want to see everything and don't yet have the experienced caver's ability to construct a passage in the mind, to see without aiming a light into every nook and cranny. Their heads are fairly steady on their necks; mine wobbles and bobs like a lollipop on a soggy stick as I swing my light everywhere I can. The passage soon brings us to a breakdown, a section strewn with fallen boulders.

Breakdowns occur because limestone fractures easily. It also dissolves easily, which explains the development of the cave in the first place. Limestone is a sedimentary rock formed in shallow seas where millions of shells that had dropped to the ocean floor were crushed under the weight of millions of other shells, compacted and pulverized, and finally pressed into stone. Layers and layers of limestone, lifted and folded by tectonic plate action and mountain-building forces, rose above those ancient seas and now lie beneath topsoils all over the world. Because groundwater is laced with a mild carbonic acid, when it seeps underground it slowly, almost imperceptibly, dissolves bits of the highly soluble limestone, creating tiny fissures that channel more and more of the water. After millions of years, the fissure becomes crevice becomes tunnel and then cavern, a whole subterranean system of streams that continue to widen and dissolve. Meanwhile, secondary formations begin to grow. A drop of groundwater trickles through the cave's ceiling and into the dank air of its interior. It hangs from the ceiling for a while, grows heavy, and then the water either evaporates or drips to the floor, leaving a precipitate on the ceiling that hardens into calcite. Drop after drop after drop, the calcite gets left behind; it grows into stalactites or stalagmites; it ripples into shieldlike formations or bubbles into cave pearls, those lustrous beads sometimes found in underwater pools.

Eventually, if water drains completely out of the cave or walls are later undercut by streams, the cave ceiling may lose its support, the limestone may begin to crack and fracture, and the roof then collapses. The result is a breakdown, a pile of debris that can be scattered over a hundred yards or heaped into fifty feet, debris that can range in size from tennis balls to houses. Of course, in the dark, you can't see them all at once. We turn and sweep the narrow beacons of our headlamps over the boulders of the breakdown we now face in the middle of this cave passage, our half-dozen small ovals of light lingering on the ceiling, darting over muddy walls, sizing up the obstacles ahead. The chunks of debris are angular, tilted, propped against one another, some with knife-ridges, others flat as altars. You *negotiate* them; you strike a bargain with their stone bodies: If I put my left foot here and use that tiny ridge as a handhold while I dig my right knee into solid stone and hoist myself up to the top, will you agree to hold still? To not break apart or roll in the midst of my clambering? If you're skillful enough, the break-down keeps its part of the bargain: It holds still while you maneuver through it. Of course, it's likely to hold still even if you're clumsy, in which case negotiation is just another term for the delusion that you've behaved correctly and been re-warded for it. It's one of the few delusions you can get away with in a cave.

We move through the breakdown slowly, carefully. Each foot is placed deliberately, the next move already deter-mined. Debbie leads me, calling out directions, showing me how to hoist my body, how to use my knees, how to lean into a boulder and inch sideways. Constantly aware of the fragil-ity of my body, I work these stones like a slow motion, 3-D hopscotch, searching out the safe foothold, the wide-enough ledge, the handhold that will keep me from falling. I forget that I'm deep inside a mountain. I forget about everything but the next move. And the next and the next and a crawling, scrambling, exhilarating, exhausting hour later, we have worked our way through. My legs are trembly, my knees ache, and I'm sure that underneath my overalls my skin has begun to bloom into bruises.

We pause for water, and Kathy says we have a choice to make. We can take a shortcut through a very narrow passage or continue on the longer, easier way. The two guys, Debbie, and Sue, a small woman, choose the shortcut. I want to look at it first. Kathy leads me around a corner and shines a light toward an impossibly small opening. It's irregular, a cleft be-tween an old jumble of rocks, maybe fourteen inches high. It twists around in there, Kathy explains matter-of-factly. It's best to go headfirst and there's a bit of a downward slope at the end. It's a torture chamber, I think, a too-small casket tilted foot-up and you're the one inside. My body tightens. It's what cavers call a flattener, a squeeze, the kind that can take the buttons off your shirt and the skin off your cheek. Every eighth of an inch matters, which might mean taking your pack off, sometimes your helmet, maybe even your clothes.

The most notorious squeezes have names: the Gun Barrel, Jam Crack, the Electric Armpit Crawl, Devil's Pinch. You can even train for them by buying a product called a Squeeze Box. It's essentially a play torture chamber for cavers, a wooden box, about thirty by thirty inches, open on the two ends. You set it up in your living room, get down on your hands and knees, and crawl through it. No problem. But the box has adjustable sides and top. You loosen the bolts, lower the lid, slide the sides closer, crawl through again. You keep doing this, keep shrinking the interior space until you find your "zone of comfortable passage." Or, as another caver puts it, your "too-tight threshold." I know one caver, about 140 pounds and five feet eight inches, who can wriggle through an opening just 7 ¾ inches high. Though a Squeeze Box may be good practice for learning how to squinch through small places, doing it on your living room carpet, within easy reach of Queen Anne–style table legs, familiar clumps of dog hair, the swath of sunlight on the floor, just doesn't duplicate what causes the panic. To simulate that, you'd have to darken the room completely, drop the temperature to 50 degrees, saturate the room with humidity, turn the wood into stone, heap a mountain over your head, and extend the length of the passage to, say, a thousand feet, like the one in Gaping Gill Cave in England that means an hour on hands and knees, no chance at all to even sit up and rest. You'd have to twist the space, make it corkscrew and descend, make the walls uneven, jutting in and out of your ribs. Either roughen up the interior so it scrapes your skin raw or smear it with mud. Eliminate all noise except for the occasional dripping of water, which echoes.

I stare at the narrow slit at my feet. Choosing this route could mean five minutes of panic-stricken me thrashing against stone. But choosing the long route around means an extra hour of climbing and butt-sliding, a sure strain on my already trembling limbs. Suddenly I want sunshine, a paved intersection with a stoplight and green arrow, oldies on the radio station—not this dark, silent world in which neither choice appeals. I squat down and look closer, try to imagine sliding my body into that stony hole.

Attempting to sail home, Odysseus approached a narrow passage of water that runs between the cave of Scylla and the whirlpool of Charybdis. He'd been warned about the strait, that on one side, the sea swirls and sucks down black water and three times a day swallows whatever comes near it. On the other, a six-headed cave monster with rows of hideous fangs preys on whoever passes by. Circe had described to him the wreckage from the whirlpool and the agony of the men swallowed by each of Scylla's mouths. She'd warned him that fighting either monster is futile and had advised him what to do. As the ship sailed toward the double danger, Odysseus paced the deck.

The story has become idiom: To be caught between Scylla and Charybdis is to be squeezed between two dangers. Avoiding one means exposing yourself to the other. How often do we find ourselves trying to choose between two risks—possible death to the entire crew or certain death to six men? Loneliness or hostility? Unkindness or dishonesty? What to do? Here, inside this mountain, taking the long route means adding an hour not just to my time, but to

Kathy's too, as she will not leave me alone in the cave. Taking the short route might mean the others have to calm a panicked novice. Fear or exhaustion? I tell Kathy I need to take the long way around.

Lunch is where we meet up again, a half-hour of rest and squashed peanut butter sandwiches and the story of Sue's moment of panic in the shortcut. Larry had preceded her down the chute and had turned to help guide her through. Not more than a couple of yards from the end, one arm extended, the other pinched to her side, her head turned sideways to fit through, she'd been seized by claustrophobia. She didn't panic, but Larry, his headlight aimed up the chute, could see the fear in her eyes. A wild-animal look, he said, something half-human caught in a rock, paralyzed in overalls and a helmet. It lasted only a few seconds. She calmed herself and was able to laugh about it over lunch. I was oddly relieved. Here was an expert caver who'd gone underground all over the world and she could still have such moments.

Mine was coming.

After another hour of climbing and crawling, we split into two groups, Kathy and I staying behind to poke around more leisurely while the others scrambled off to find a further passage. Kathy wants to show me some small rimstone pools just up a small incline. Miniature dams on a miniature terraced hillside, they look like an aerial scene from a film of the Indian countryside. A little further up the incline I see a cleft in the stone. A tight passage, Kathy says, but short, maybe fifteen feet. You're on your belly but there's still a good four inches above your head. I want to try it, I tell her. Away from the others, Kathy's calm presence nearby, I want to do it. Kathy hesitates and then leads me up, describes it again, pointing out that if she goes first I'll see her light on the other end. It'll be something clear to scooch toward. She wiggles through in fifteen seconds with no trouble. I start through with no trouble.

I get a third of the way in. I'm on my belly, arms stretched out ahead. I can move my head, lift it slightly to look for the end, lay it sideways on the floor, inch forward with my hands and elbows, but I have to stay flat on my belly. I can't sit up or draw my knees up close to my chest, which is what I suddenly want to do.

How to explain it? Some curtain falls, blocks off your ability to be rational. I stop where I am, head turned sideways, staring at the passage wall. I'm pretty sure Kathy's talking to me but my heart's pounding far louder than her calm voice, which sounds muffled now, trying to get through to me who's halfway out of a nightmare, the sheets wrapped around my face, the air thick with dread, only these sheets are made of stone and I can't claw them away from my face, can't even get my hands close to my face. My body's instinct to run is suddenly distended, swollen, flooding every available place in my mind. It's a wordless instinct, thoughtless, incapable of negotiation, completely oblivious to the tiny part of my shrunken mind that sends out one last gasping word of restraint—*wait, wait*—to sweep recklessly through the body, which wants immediately to heed the new command: *run, run.* I try to bend my right leg, as if readying for a sprint, but my knee smashes immediately into the wall. It's as if I'm in a full-body straitjacket shoved headfirst into a too-small casing inside solid stone.

I think Kathy's still talking to me. I can see her headlamp, but it's not the welcome light at the end of a tunnel; it's the light of a train barreling toward me, who's blocking all the space with my body. The stones have begun to edge closer, the ceiling to lower, and I look at Kathy again and, miraculously, I hear her say, "Take a deep breath." She says it in the same tone she might offer me orange juice, a poached egg for breakfast. I close my eyes and breathe, picture the air filling my lungs, feel my chest expand and then drop, imagine the exhaled air keeping the walls at bay. I breathe again. I will my limbs to be still.

The best advice for managing a squeeze comes from Buddhism. The squeeze, Buddhists say, is the unbearable place. The place that makes us want, more than anything else, to be elsewhere. The uncomfortable, embarrassing place where the irrational, the fearful, the panicking parts of ourselves want out, to jump ship, to leave. Buddhists are talking, of course, about mental squeezes, when one part of the mind presents us with irrefutable evidence of something another part of the mind absolutely will not acknowledge. What to do? The usual reaction is to suppress one part and carry on as if it doesn't exist, meaning something in us shrinks. It's a strategy we resort to often. Getting a little smaller, after all, means gaining a little more wiggle room. Now maybe we can squirm another inch, sidle sideways, slip out of the crack. But if we're tired of shrinking in the grip of a real squeeze, denial doesn't work anymore and all the evidence becomes palpable: You can't live with him and you can't live without him. About the one big thing, you know if you say yes, disaster follows; if you say no, catastrophe. There's no more forward and there's no backward. There's a rock in front of your face and there's a rock digging into your back.

Study the rock, the Buddhists say. Open your eyes and study the rock that's pressing into your nose. Look at its color. Note the variations in texture. Breathe. If you can get your glove off, feel it. Muddy? Sandy? A bit of slime? What, exactly, is pressing into your back? Is it ridged or smooth or lumpy? Where, exactly, does it press? Into your shoulder blades, your bum, your ribs? These are impossible tasks, and they're exactly what a Buddhist would say about being caught in a squeeze. Study the place. Watch how your mind leaps to absurdities. Watch the way panic looms and recedes. You're not going anywhere at the moment, so you might as well be curious about where you are.

I open my eyes. In front of me is a damp wall of bedrock. Dark brown, grayish, a thin skim of viscous mud. A few inches up, the wall's pebbly surface shows through. Small craters and crust, a little more tan, speckled. This is limestone, I know, the primary rock in which caves form. I'm lying in a small tunnel, I tell myself, in which the stone has been dissolved, so what's left here, crowding me, has to be less soluble than what's gone. I try to see the tunnel itself, and the room behind me that we just left, try to picture the breakdown we crossed through before lunch, the ceiling above it, the mountain above that, the valley we drove through to get here, the sinkholes and disappearing streams so typical of karst, this landscape of pocked and riddled limestone. A book I have at home flashes through my mind —photographs of karst landscapes all over the world, in England and New Zealand, in China and New Mexico, their deep pits and sunken bowls and, underneath, their caverns and tunnels, like this one I'm frozen in. I turn my head sideways on the floor to rest. I breathe, I hear Kathy's voice, I hear Rilke's voice: *Everything close to my face is stone.* In a squeeze, perspective is difficult; alternatives and denial are impossible. Sociability is a joke, dishonesty an enormous waste of time. At the worst of it, every trick for getting out of a tight spot fails. And, Rilke says, if your experience with grief is limited and about to deepen, the darkness feels oppressive, the agent of diminishment.

Odysseus lingered at the entrance to the passage. To drown or risk being devoured? To go down with his ship or to sacrifice a few? In the end, Odysseus did as Circe advised: He passed through on Scylla's side of the strait. Scylla saw them coming, of course, twisted her six heads down to the ship and plucked six men from the deck. Odysseus saw them lifted, writhing, into the air, their twelve legs flailing as they disappeared down her throats. He did what commanders-in-chief do in every major battle. He did what court systems and schools do, what each of us does in large and small decisions a dozen times a year: Forced to choose between two dangers, he chose the certain deaths of a few over the probable deaths of many. We do it all our lives. We reject small parts of ourselves, which then die—unexpressed dreams, secret longings, the hopes we say were minor once we've chosen to discard them.

The Odyssey is the quintessential Western hero's story, full of agonizing choices and ordeals. The hero makes all the right moves and eventually gets home again. His adventures teach us about the indomitable human spirit, about courage, perseverance, and the need to make hard choices. I raise my head. My helmet bangs immediately against the ceiling. A warning, I think, lowering it slowly. That Odysseus lost dozens of men in the process and kept his wife waiting for twenty years are chalked up as the acceptable losses one incurs on a heroic quest.

Were there alternatives? Odysseus couldn't avoid the Scylla versus Charybdis passage entirely; it was way too late to turn around and find another route home. But I want to know how Western thought would be different if Odysseus had lived a little later, been able to read a bit of Buddhism before he set sail. Caught between two dangers, what if he'd heeded the Buddhist advice, lowered his sails, and studied the passage between them? Why couldn't he have waited, spent a few days timing Charybdis' thrice-daily thrashings?

Why would a delay of a few more days matter in a ten-year odyssey? It seems he could have charted the pauses, understood the pattern, and then steered his boat to that side of the passage during a lull and avoided Scylla altogether.

The trouble with a squeeze, Odysseus knew and I know, is that it imparts a certain urgency. We think we can't stand being caught between a rock and hard place, can't stand it one more second, and so we flail our way out, bruised and panicky. To resist the panic, to wait until the mind can consider more carefully, just to wait at all, in fact, requires patience and a tolerance for boredom, neither of which makes for the high drama of legends. No wonder Odysseus bolted.

A diagram in a cave rescue document flashes through my mind. It shows a caver caught in a vertical crevice. Her left arm is stretched up, as if reaching toward the rescuer at the top who leans over and shines his light down into the crack. Her right arm is pinned to her side, straight down. Her head is turned to the side. The two crevice walls squeeze her the whole length of her back, her rear, her knees, her chest. She can't breathe well. Her feet dangle. There's nothing below them. Her only possible course of action is to stay calm and completely still while others work their ropes and harnesses. To squirm at all is to risk slipping further down. In fact, any movement on her part will only jeopardize her position. I'm suddenly grateful for the stone my body's stretched on. I lift my head carefully, turn it to the right, wiggle the toe of my right boot a bit, feel how firm the cave floor is beneath me. Breathe.

Ten years ago, about to enter a cave for the first time, I might have read the wrong things to my young creative writing students. Or to myself. Instead of myth and metaphor, maybe we should have studied mud and rock, studied the literal in front of our faces for a while, let the figurative emerge on its own. It does. It will. I might have avoided panic, gotten through that squeeze, been able to follow my students into that cave; might have been able to sit with them in an underground room and learn something about stone fissures, cave minerals, how sediment weathers underground. Kathy's reminding me to breathe. I twist my head toward her; I inhale and count to ten and know something else that might also be true: No matter how many physically bigger guides precede me or how many times I squirm through a squeeze, it might be this hard. There's a rock pressing into my back, a rock in front of my face, and nothing to do but look at it, slow down my breath, my urge to flee. I will my hands to unclench, raise a gloved finger and run it slowly down the dimpled surface of stone.

2

BEGIN HERE

The stone's alive with what's invisible.

— SEAMUS HEANEY

ON A THREE-INCH STRIP of orange tape, somebody has scrawled the words "begin here." The tape is attached on one end to a stone wall at least fifty yards inside this pitch-black cave in western Maryland; the other end dangles limply. There's no breeze to make it flutter. In fact, you'd never even see it if you weren't looking for it or if your light didn't happen to land on it, as mine did.

The handwriting on the tape is no help—no indication of gender, age, origin, or profession. The tape itself is fairly bright, like the new survey tape you see tied to stakes along property lines in new developments. Part of a new mapping project? I doubt it, as this cave was well surveyed many years ago. Its main passages and side passages, familiar to most local cavers, are carefully drawn on maps almost any-one can obtain. I'd studied one before I came in and, having noted that the passages split partway in and that the left passage becomes a skinny ledge above a crevice, had stayed to the right. The traverses in here have been measured, the ceiling heights determined, the squeezes and vertical drops marked. Why would anyone start a new map? Not likely, either, that the tape marks the starting point of some caving competition. The image of cavers in bulky coveralls and helmets, bent over in starting positions, bolting into the dark as soon as the pistol cracks, sprinting along corridors and bounding through breakdowns, would be incongruous. Cavers are a wisely cautious group of people, and speed would be not only foolish but also unappealing. More likely they'd be moseying along, pausing to hunt for cave crickets or fossils.

Begin here. Perhaps a clue in a treasure hunt set up just for cavers, a modern fantasy search for Aladdin's lamp, supposedly found in the legendary Cave of Wonders. Or a search for hidden riches? History books are full of stories of fortune seekers scouring caves in which pirates supposedly buried their loot. On Cocos Island off of Costa Rica, hordes of them have headed into coastal caves with water-stained maps and metal detectors, searching for clues that would lead them to the eleven Spanish privateers' booty allegedly stashed there in the seventeenth century. What kind of clues did they look for? Diggings in the floor? Charred walls that might indicate a campfire? Bits of metal? Soggy slabs from treasure chests? I picture them far back in a cave turning over a scrap of something, trying to figure out what, if anything, it meant, whether to keep going or give up or find some more telling hint.

How to know whether this bit of orange tape means anything or not? Someone went to a lot of effort: got the gate key from the Nature Conservancy, which owns this cave, hiked up a steep ridge, crawled back into the cave, found some way to affix a piece of plastic to a muddy stone wall. Dropping hints, leaving clues—I love the kind of puzzle they imply. *Begin here.* I search farther down the passage but don't, of course, know what I'm looking for.

Bruce Smith, who has spent years tracking cave clues he hopes will lead to other treasures more important than booty and magical wishes, shares my need to piece together an incomplete story. So do Amy Frappier and Christopher Henshilwood. And Hazel Barton and Nancy Aulenbach. Scores of people, it turns out, are willing to spend a good portion of their professional lives on their hands and knees in the dark searching for clues, for certain calcified minerals, bone fragments, and trickles of water.

An archaeobotanist who studies cave artifacts, Bruce is a tall man, broad-shouldered and big-chested, the kind of relaxed guy who shrugs his shoulders a lot and smiles easily. He must wear at least a size 13 boot. When I met him several months ago in his Smithsonian Institution office, I tried to imagine him where I've been, squirming in a cave, those big hands pulling him through a narrow passage or digging in a cave for artifacts, and wondered aloud whether his equanimity ever disintegrates into claustrophobia. "No," he shrugged, "not a chance. I haven't even been through a tight squeeze." I didn't know whether to admire him or to be suspicious.

He handed me one of the clues he's been collecting for years—a five-hundred-year-old peduncle that's been buried for half a millennium in a Mexican cave. Uncovered about forty years ago, it's an inch and a half long, three-quarters of an inch wide. A mottled brown cross between a dried piece of fruit and an old wooden carving, this peduncle—squash stem—is a piece of the puzzle to which Bruce has devoted his research. In front of us was a large table, and on top of it was a cardboard box crammed with small zip-top plastic bags, each with a peduncle inside and a tiny piece of paper with a number scrawled in pencil. Bruce opened a drawer under the table and pulled out more plastic bags, each with a single squash stem, all of them part of a large collection of peduncles uncovered in caves and now stored in the Smithsonian in cardboard boxes.

How, I wondered, did he know to look in caves in the first place? I've seen a bit of scat in caves, a few salamanders, a few bones, lots of mud, lots of gritty-dry rock. A feather once. And a couple of sticks. Debris, mostly, like the dregs and lint —old tissues, ticket stubs, pen caps—you find in the pockets of your jeans on laundry day. I'm not used to thinking of caves—wild caves, anyway—as depositories for much of anything you'd go looking for, except, perhaps, dripping calcite. In fact, quite the opposite: I've thought of them as rather barren places, their insides emptied out, their rooms vacant. Not at all the kind of place I'd go hunting for clues.

But others do. Bruce unzipped another bag and rolled into my hand another peduncle and another scrap of paper, this one marked TC50/41-2, meaning it was found at Level 2 in Coxcatlan Cave in Oaxaca, Mexico. Other peduncles were found at other levels in other caves, under hundreds of years of sand and powdery dirt, pebbles and rocks, and from all over the world, from the hidden recesses of Grotta dell'Uzzo in Sicily, from Ulu Leang Cave in Indonesia, from the dark pockets of the Tamaulipas Mountains of northern Mexico. Bruce needs not just peduncles from such places, but also squash seeds, ancient corncobs, and gourd rinds. He needs beans and pollen grains, root remnants and sunflower seeds, any organic evidence from those caverns that might help him study the origins of domesticated corn.

I have great respect for the hide-and-seek world in which Bruce works, for its power to make a person more foolish or more alert. Maybe both. By the time I was nine or ten, I'd taken to hiding things in the woods behind our house. A few twigs, for example, into which I'd first carefully cut a diagonal slant or a series of notches. Or sometimes I'd peel off a spiral of bark and then push the marked wood beneath a rotten log. Or pebbles, which I pretended were the notes of some song I'd position above me on level branches or below me on top of small boulders. Sometimes I laid out a simple melody of stones among the blades of grass under the clothesline: CABFG or an A-minor chord. I'd watch my mother stand there, pinning wet sheets to the line, and wonder whether she could feel the secret beneath her feet. Of course I'd forget where in the woods I'd stashed the things, and of course they became mostly unfindable in the twiggy, weedy, rock-strewn woods. I loved to walk there a week later imagining some could be under my foot, others just above me. They could be anywhere, and I began to sense what was possible in this life.

You don't tell others you do such things. About the quirky gestures most of us make in our private worlds, we keep quiet. It's not just that those gestures seem stupid or too revealing of a certain oddness; it's that in the shared world of family or friends, they get stripped of their value. We keep them secret as a way of defining our private world. I told Jeanne, however, who was, like me, a shy child, fond of books and the private bower beneath a tree. When we were twelve, I told her about the pebbles and twigs and she nodded solemnly, and I knew then that I could tell her all kinds of things and that I didn't have to. "Moss," she said, "and what you can tuck under moss at the foot of a tree." I nodded solemnly. "The secret of the world is hidden in the world," Claude Lévi-Strauss once said. And now, years later, now that Jeanne's dying looms and recedes and no medical breakthrough or human love can affect its course, this is even truer: The intrigue of secrets is often complicated by our helplessness to unravel them.

Pebbles under moss. A piece of tape in a cave. Maybe a peduncle or geode, claw marks on a tree, a bone that signals premature death, or chunks of calcite that reveal a whole history of ancient hurricanes. That's what Amy Frappier's looking for in caves. Not bits of plant life, but evidence of storms. She needs large things, things she crawls into Central American caves with a hammer and chisel to retrieve. A graduate of the Institute for the Study of Earth, Oceans, and Space at the University of New Hampshire (UNH), Amy was originally interested in climate change, not caves. "In fact," she told me, "the only cave I even knew of as a child was a local one all the parents had warned us about." A smugglers' lair, the kids had been told, not a place to venture into. Today she emerges from the caves of Belize lugging three-foot-long stalactites and stalagmites that she packages in bubble wrap and ships to the lab at UNH. Concerned about cave conservation, she selects only the most inconspicuous formations she can find, hoping the destruction she causes will be compensated by the knowledge the samples yield. Back at the lab, she carefully slices them open with a rock saw and shaves off tiny fragments. She's looking for evidence of the kind of rainwater that dripped millions of years ago into the dark, subterranean caves of Belize, those sunless crannies sheltered from rain and sky, from clouds and weather fronts sweeping across Central America.

Here's why: Oxygen has two major isotopes, one heavy and one light. The lighter isotopes will evaporate before the heavier ones, so a hurricane, whose winds cause a lot of evaporation, tends to pull a lot of light oxygen into its swirl. Furthermore, a rainstorm will drop any heavier isotopes first so that by the time a mature hurricane hits land, it's raining very "light" water. When this lighter water seeps into the ground, percolates into the cave below, and gets trapped into stalagmites, it should be detectable millions of years later in a spectrometer. A person studying those isotopes, then, ought to be able graph patterns of when and how frequently long-ago hurricanes pelted the ground above the cave.

Other cave clues to ancient history: High on a South African cliff overlooking the Indian Ocean, Christopher Henshilwood and his group of archaeologists searching in Blombos Cave uncovered two 77,000-year-old chunks of red ocher —iron ore—into which had been etched a series of overlapping triangles. Their find created ripples all across the world. That the etchings are geometric, not representational—no foliage or cloud patterns, no animal or mineral shapes—is important because geometry signals abstract thinking.

There are even clues in underwater caves. Because of the IMAX movie *Amazing Caves,* they're famous now, Hazel Barton and Nancy Aulenbach, cave divers who are probably the most intrepid of all those who hunt cave secrets. They enter the double unknown: deep water that hides the entrance to an underwater cave. They fasten helmets, zip up dive suits, and shoulder underwater video cameras, sterile collecting bags, canisters of liquid nitrogen, oxygen tanks, batteries, saws, chisels, and trowels. They dive into a dark pool, squirm through the crevice at the bottom, and into the sunless and flooded labyrinth under the jungles of Mexico. They breaststroke underground, sometimes for hours at a time, looking for the place between inland jungle and ocean, where fresh water mingles with salt water and forms a shimmery layer known as a halocline.

Picture a column of water. The top layer is fresh water from aboveground rains that have seeped into the cave. The bottom is seawater that has infiltrated the caves from the ocean. In between the top and bottom layers floats the halocline. It's in this layer, microbiologists speculate, that a whole host of microbes nobody's ever seen might exist. Extremophiles, they're called, bacteria that can live only in the extreme dark or cold, unknown bugs, multicelled beings, some with tentacled stumps and nicknames like moss piglets, that the cave divers collect in their vials and canisters as evidence of previously unknown life forms.

What are they all looking for? What puzzle pieces are these, these cave-hidden peduncles and stalagmites and extremophiles? Clues to the past? Or to the future? Both, Bruce says. His particular interest is the emergence of agriculture in Mesoamerica. Establishing the age of plant artifacts matters not only for Bruce's research into the beginning of domesticated crops, but also for how that look into the past might, like the study of cave microbes and carbon in stalagmites, help us in the future. Agricultural botanists looking at those same ancient plant parts, for example, want to know what preceded them, what corn looked like before humans selected their biggest seeds, their fattest kernels, and began a program of selective breeding. This is the question they're trying to answer: What, in evolutionary terms, preceded the vegetables now displayed on modern grocery shelves? What did they look like when they grew wild and unmanipulated by human beings? These researchers, too, head into the caves to search for cobs and seeds of smaller, undomesticated corn.

What they find there might someday save the agricultural world from ruin. Archaeobotanists are studying teosinte, the suspected ancestor of corn, to find what was wild enough in its genes two thousand years ago to fend off disease, the ravages of drought, the small sucking mouths of insects. Like so much else in the plant and animal worlds, the strengths of today's domesticated corn—its reliability and its plumpness —are also its weakness. Bred specifically for those very qualities, the plant has lost its ability to resist disease, to fend off infestation. These are the worries that fuel agribusiness's interest in Bruce Smith's research.

Amy's work in the caves is a warning too, an attempt to predict the future by looking at the past. Back in her lab at UNH, bent over microscopes for hours and hours, she's hunting not just for information about hurricanes of the far past and El Niño effects of the near past, but also about how past patterns might help foretell future patterns. Is global warming really a new trend? Might there be evidence in the caves to suggest such warmings are cyclical? And if global warming increases hurricane frequency, is that incentive enough to decrease our current use of fossil fuels?

From the chunks of iron ore found in the South African cave: the intriguing idea that humans in this part of the world were capable of abstract thought and art long before anthropologists had previously thought. The possibility has sent hundreds of investigators back into the old Spanish and French caves and dozens more scaling the African cliffs in search of undiscovered ones, fueling the debates between those who'd found evidence of what they thought was the earliest modern human behavior in the 40,000-year-old excavated layers of Eurasian caves and those who had recently been digging in the older, dry sands of South African caves.

And from those underwater caves, newly discovered life forms with a wide range of genetic diversity may, like the discovery of penicillin from cheese molds years ago, lead one day to new antibiotics and advances in cancer treatments.

Fragile clues from fragile environments, both of which can be fatally compromised by careless human incursion.

Anything we do inside them, no matter how noble our intentions, threatens the delicate balance of temperature and humidity and food, the centuries of slow-growing formations. I'm not opposed to scientists probing our planets, our brains, the insides of our eyeballs or our undergrounds, but I also don't want the cave completely unroofed, its pockets turned inside out and picked clean. If cave exploration is a treasure hunt, not just for hidden things but for knowledge of the hidden, then it probably requires the most judicious and gentle removal of clues, a lot of bubble-wrapping of artifacts and careful trodding. Only those who move carefully and watch awhile before they stir up too much silt will likely spot the smallest giveaways, the subtlest changes in temperature, shifts in weight, the shimmer of halocline between fresh and ocean waters. Clues, in other words, that need to be coaxed, urged, evoked, or seduced. I want the cave diver with tiny vials and a lot of patience, the cave archaeologist with the precision tool, the tasteful wrist-twist of removal and slow sorting of fiber from clod.

And I want some small hint about this bit of orange tape sixty feet belowground, whose significance continues to escape me. I leave it finally and head farther into the cave. I'd been told there are isopods in this cave, small creatures that live deep in the cave's darkness. I've never seen them, but know they're less than a half-inch long, bullet-shaped, white, and aquatic. Along the uneven floor runs a small stream. In most places, there's just enough room between the water and the wall for a boot. For a half hour or so, I straddle the cave's stream and, in an awkward side-to-side gait, try to keep my big feet from squashing any stream troglobites. My flashlight, trained on the water, reveals only pebbles. Finally, tired and a bit bored, I sit down in the dark beside the stream, turn off the flashlight, take off my helmet, and let its lamp shine up on the cave walls, a large circle of pale yellow floating against rocky juts and deep cracks. At its periphery, the yellow pales to cream and then ivory, and there in the flimsy light-edge of water swim one and then three, four tiny white things, like fat rice or small onion slivers. When I aim my light directly on them, they slip under pebbles, gone; the stream runs clear and empty. They hate the light. Born in the wet darkness, they must feel my lamp as we might a sun bearing down, heat and brightness, a thing to run from or be ruined by. I aim the light up, try flicking it toward and away, back and forth across the streambed, learning how the darkness elicits them. As perhaps it does other things half-hidden in a cave, coaxing them from invisibility to significance. Is it the setting itself that seems to transform its creatures, its bits of stone and seed, from mere flotsam into fragments of a larger story? Maybe that's what has me thinking now that everything in here might be a clue to something else.

The temperature feels like low 50s. Caves maintain a constant temperature year-round, one that's close to the annual mean temperature of the surrounding area. That stability is one of the factors that make the cave such a good museum. This cave is high on a ridge in the plateau region of the Appalachian Mountains where the mean hovers around 48 degrees. So it makes sense that I'd feel cooler in here than I have in other caves where temperatures have been more typically in the mid to high 50s. The humidity's high, too. My glasses keep fogging up, and I think of what underground waterfalls can indicate about the geology above them. And then of the telltale smell of sulfur in a cave, the sound of cave-echoes, the sights of unburied basketry bits and mummy cloth and fossils. More clues? From that last strenuous stretch of crawling, steam rises from my knees, and I remember reading how smoke from a New England cave led a posse to a counterfeiter's lair. I could make myself crazy with such wondering. How do we know if what we're looking at even matters? Whether it's a clue to anything larger or next or nothing at all?

Days later I ask a caving friend about the orange tape. "Isopod study," he answers. A biologist he knows from the next county over is researching the population and extent of their habitat in that cave and uses orange tape to mark off beginnings and endings of sections for counting. He's evidently interested in them as indicator species of the health of that stream and maybe the effects of nearby mining. Or perhaps he doesn't know what he's looking for, but hopes some finding will lead to another finding that might someday matter.

Agricultural diversity, cyclical weather patterns, the origins of human abstract thinking, extremophilic medicines — big theories, all of them, and all of them needing the small bits of stone, fiber, mineral, and cells tucked in some of the world's great hiding places. In other caves, pottery shards and bones, the Dead Sea Scrolls, cave paintings and stones that don't belong there. Illuminated manuscripts and church icons, evidence, even, that small communities took refuge inside from religious and political persecutors.

Why didn't I find the orange tape that said "Stop here"? Surely if the biologist has marked off the beginning point for study, he's marked the end point too. Maybe I hadn't gone far enough. That cave, the longest in Maryland, has over four thousand feet of passages, and I hadn't explored even a fourth of them. Or maybe, like countless others searching for things in a cave, I'd mistaken a crucial clue for a bit of litter. Or simply missed it. Easy to do. When it comes to searching for clues, I'm learning that no secret pocket, no backyard tree, no beneath-the-bed box can pose more obstacles and opportunities than a cave does. Creviced, often narrow, abrasively dry or slimy-wet, a cave deters any searcher accustomed to sunlight, safety, and the ease of walking upright. It's a hideout full of nooks and crannies, low ceilings, confusing side passages, and the sequestered's most important refuge: eternal darkness.

3

THE TWILIGHT ZONE

The seat of the soul is there, where the outer
and inner worlds meet.
— NOVALIS

IN THE AREA of a cave between the entrance and the dark, a little sunlight filters in, but mostly it's gray here in the twilight zone, the rocks faintly outlined. From where I'm standing, I can look down and to the right, farther into the cave, and see how the black gets denser, takes on substance, fills in every crack. Or I can look up, to the left, and still see, not sky, but at least the brown rocks and obvious handholds, small protrusions, even an insect in the air. I keep my eye on it, and on the stone bumps I could use to climb out. Even as I take another step back, I'm trying to memorize escape. This is the place of the in-between. In between light and dark, between the aboveground and belowground, the limbo land. It isn't fear I feel here, which would propel me out. It's a foreboding of nothing I can name, and so fleeing seems dumb. It's a disquiet I can counter only by flinching away from the nothing and toward the walls, which I keep touching and leaning against.

On a hot summer day like this one, the twilight zone is a convoluted, dimly lit, air-conditioned refuge. Salamanders wait in the rock pockets here, a few daddy longlegs scurry away from our lights, cave crickets cling to the walls. Here and there lie what might have been small piles of scat, raccoon maybe, or pack rat. In the cave's high humidity, they're coated with fungus, blooming like miniature clumps of white cotton candy on the cave floor.

As in most caves, this twilight zone is inhabited by two kinds of creatures: troglophiles, meaning "cave lovers," and trogloxenes. The former need a dark, damp environment, which might be a cave but could also be a rotten log or tree stump. Some individual troglophiles may spend their whole lives in caves, but others can complete their entire life cycles outside the cave. Or they may travel in and out. Beetles are an example, as are earthworms and some salamanders. Trogloxenes—from the Latin words for "cave" and "stranger"—are creatures that often take refuge in a cave, away from heat or cold or fierce storms. Or they are, like me, drawn by something inexplicable. Bears, of course, den in the twilight zone, curled in small alcoves, giving birth in midwinter to cubs who for two or three months know only the dark and semidark, the low ceilings and stony walls. Bats spend hot summer days here, and skunks and raccoons and frogs will come here to escape the extremes of the outside world. Pack rats haul in their treasured bits of foil, their gum wrappers and soft-drink tops, but no trogloxenes stay in a cave. They can't. They're not adapted to total darkness and can't survive on the meager food supply. They hang out in the entrances and twilight zones, but they leave the cave for richer food supplies, for possible mates, for a little sunshine, returning for its protection, traveling back and forth as their appetites and comforts demand.

It hadn't been comfort or appetite I'd felt an hour ago, standing above the entrance to Devil's Hole just thirty miles from my home in western Maryland. Staring at it, I couldn't get rid of the image of a half-opened mouth, its stone lips twisted, almost curled. Something about that fissure evoked the same tug and revulsion I've felt being wheeled into operating rooms when I knew the benefits of the surgery even as I also knew there was still time to get up, untie the hospital gown, and walk away, the same way I could unfasten my helmet, step out of my coveralls, get back in the car, and drive home. But something's wrong, maybe broken or a little disarranged inside; I'm perplexed by my initial cave terror, I don't know how to handle Jeanne's dying, and I've been telling myself I have to do this, have to go through with it, have to go on in so I can come back out, the body or the psyche better realigned.

Maybe it's not a mouth. Maybe it's a wound that can't heal. Or won't. The jumbled rocks around its entrance resemble picked-off scabs; the raised, irregular debris, the dark clotted matter that sometimes surrounds an unclean gash in the skin. I knew I'd have to touch them, hold onto them in order to slide and climb down to the bottom of the sink.

I kept the chin strap fastened and moved closer to the opening, which is framed with things I love: ferns, trillium, the lush green mosses softening the stone entrance. If they weren't inviting enough, then there was the air that comes out of a cave. It promised relief on this hot and humid August day when four of us had hiked a half mile or so across an open field to reach the cave and arrived with our shirts soaked in sweat. Liz, Ron, and Rich are friends of mine, biologists I know not just from campus but also from Gandalf's, the local café that caters to artists, aging hippies, and vegetarians. They scrambled down the sink first, eager for what they knew was the coolness wafting out of the entrance. They stood down there at the cave's mouth, gulping air and water as I half-slid, half-climbed down into the sink and felt the sudden coolness, as sudden as if someone had just opened a freezer door. Devil's Hole, it turns out, isn't hot at all.

But it was a test. The entrance itself is a vertical shaft about twelve feet deep. Not a clean, smooth shaft, but a conglomerate of small spaces, some angled, some jutted, some just down. I looked down for only a second and then around at the delicate fronds, at moss that feels like a baby's hair. I was trying to memorize green.

Liz went in first, using rope and a technique called "chimneying." It's a method based on the belief that you can press your back and feet hard enough against the opposite sides of the inside chimney walls to keep yourself from falling. Picture your body as a wedge going down the chimney that keeps the walls from collapsing toward each other. You have to believe certain things about the body to do this: that you're, literally, long enough and strong enough to hold a stance of expansion rather than contraction, that you can make yourself big as you go down the hole, as opposed to small, which will be necessary later on.

I swallowed my fear, didn't tell them I thought this was crazy, concentrated instead on fiddling with the switch on my headlamp. By now I'd purchased some of my own caving equipment: helmet, lamp, kneepads I hoped would save me from the profusion of bruises from my first trips in. Simple cotton gloves that provide protection and a bit of warmth while still flexible enough for the fingers to work their way into the tiny crevices of a climb. I'd considered the heavy coveralls most cavers wear and had chosen the cheaper option—sturdy pants, old sweatshirts, a layer of polypropylene. You can spend a fortune on caving equip-

ment, I'd discovered. Carbide lamps, rappelling and ascend-
ing gear, seat and chest harnesses, cave packs with pockets
for extra batteries and water bottles, survey tools and emergency space blankets to prevent hypothermia. And even if
they aren't expensive, the recommended items accumulate:
pliers for repairs, penknife, compass, survey tape to mark a
route, first-aid kit, emergency snack food, zip-top plastic
bags for carrying out human waste; the list goes on and on.
But because I'd been making short trips, I could travel
lightly, taking only the required three sources of light, water,
pen and notebook in a plastic bag, and a candy bar. And, of
course, the indispensable helmet and its strapped-on battery
light, with which I finally stopped toying.

My turn. I sat down and dangled my legs over the edge of
the hole, and then, clinging to the rope, stretched my legs out
toward the opposite wall. Four inches shy. I wiggled closer to
the edge, stretched them farther. No contact. I knew they'd
reach as soon as I eased my rear off the lip, but I wanted
them touching the far wall before that; I wanted them touching when I could still feel stable. I hadn't made my body do
such things since I was ten and twisting myself around the
monkey bars of a school playground. The others were pa-
tient and encouraging. "Just a little more," Liz called up from
down below. "You're doing fine." I admire Liz and, seized by
a sudden wish not to disappoint her, I scooched my rear off
the edge, felt my weight on the rope for just a second and
then the firmness of the stone against my outstretched feet.
Pushing with my feet, I swung back just a bit, and sure
enough, there was the wall behind me, just where Liz said it
would be. I inched my feet down the opposite wall and
scooted my back down the wall behind me, pushing hard
with both, as if only my body kept these two walls apart. The
stones are pocked and jagged there, as if some giant cat with

ferocious claws had scratched, plucked, and shredded the stone nap, left it here to dig and scrape against my back as I slid a little farther down. I ripped my pants in the first few minutes. The ground was still ten feet below me. I was struck by the irony of the proverbial advice that in a difficult moment, one should take a deep breath, exhale slowly, relax, let the body go soft. If I'd followed that advice just then, I'd have slipped immediately to the bottom of the crevice. Keep up the pressure, I told myself. Feet against one wall, butt pushing against the other. Down farther and finally I let go of the rope as my feet touched the cave floor that then drops down in a series of ledges, like cascading stone waterfalls. I climbed down them, trying to get out of Rich's and Ron's way as they started to maneuver down the entrance.

There's still some daylight here; it spills down the well and dissipates in the crevice, creating shadows and an eerie dimming, as if the lower I drop and scrape into the earth, the more something above me very slowly closes down. Half crawling, half scooching, I move back toward the far limit of the twilight zone, into the area where, if I turn off my light, I have to wait for my eyes to adjust and, even then, I can just make out the ledges and walls, the big out-juttings above the drop-offs. If there are small critters nearby, I can't yet see them in the almost-dark. They've probably receded to nooks and crannies, wormed their way under rocks.

Life in this cave depends on them, these troglophiles and trogloxenes, and it's here in the twilight zone where they do their crucial work. They are the messengers from the outside world who bring in the news in the form of energy. From the aboveground forests and fields, from their nights of forage and scavenging and mating, they return to the cave, their bodies full of organic material. In their fur, beneath their scales, on their wings, in their tiny jaws they carry seeds, small larvae, microscopic eggs, a dismembered leg, an occasional dead body. They have dirt between the pads of their paws, on the tips of their many legs, on the backs of their feet, dirt that conceals microscopic organisms, bacteria, leaf-bits, the organic minutiae that can mean the difference between hunger and satiation for the beetles and spiders and crickets that must wait deeper in the cave for the day's delivery.

The twilight zone is the place of exchange, the marketplace where things trucked in from the outside country get dribbled, shed, or excreted. What isn't completely consumed by the creature who brought it in is left in the twilight zone to become the cave's version of meals-on-heels, meals-on-wings, meals-on-fur, without which the slow, often-blind creatures confined to the cave could not survive. As in any place of scant resources, the signaling system is on high alert in a cave; it's not long before the resident crickets and beetles move in to swarm over the leavings. If it's a small carcass, a mouse for example, that's been brought in by a skunk, the hungry ones quickly reduce it to thin bones and tiny skull. If a body hasn't been picked clean, fungi colonize it, sprouting their white and gray tufts of hair—a feast, in turn, for the blind isopods who move in and tap their way over the decay, their small mouths munching in the fuzz.

"Where do I put my left hand?" I can hear Ron ask. He is, evidently, still only partway down the chimney, though I've moved too far back in the twilight zone to see any of them. "Lower, to your right," Liz calls up, and I picture Ron in the cleft in his blue coveralls, the green above him at the cave entrance, the way he must be leaning, stretching, his left hand reaching down the pitted wall, searching for a ledge, some place to grab onto. I move farther back, my headlamp back on, searching for salamanders. Waiting in the dimming light for the others, I grow more aware of myself in a cave. Entrances are usually challenges and the mind is preoccupied with getting the body in safely. Farther in, the blackness of the dark zones absorbs the sense of self. You become the thing with the flashlight. But here in the in-between, in this prolonged stay in the twilight zone, I can see my own arms in the dim light, see my boots, my gloved hands. I'm aware of my body in a crevice belowground, can think about the fact that I'm about to disappear into the dark. The thickening blackness to my right feels like a curtain. I don't know if I'm about to go on stage or off. Whatever lines I should have memorized are gone. Green and escape have become disembodied, no longer a route to safety.

If Novalis is right, if the seat of the soul is where the inner and outer worlds meet, then surely the twilight zone of the cave is the physical correlate. Here the dark world seeps up from below, climbs up a hole to pool and linger while the light world spills down from above, its beams bending, weakening, fading. Two worlds meet in the gray, in the mix of stale air and fresh, in the overlap of cave-world and day-world. Organic material transported by wind or small streams or the backs of creatures is deposited in the pale light. Creatures from the farther recesses of the cave emerge, devour, transform it into the fuels that allow them to keep on living.

When I was a child, nine or ten, I spent hours poking holes in the dirt on the banks of the stream behind our house. The earth was soft there; I could take a small stick and use it like an awl to poke a skinny well, three inches deep, into which I'd shove pebbles, bits of fern, a wisp of hair from my brush. I thought of these tidbits as gifts to whatever might be burrowing around belowground, something that might poke its pointed head through the dirt and into the bottom of my small well and find it crammed with surprises. Even before I knew much about moles, I believed there were beings belowground that we could never see; and later, in the stage of my life when I turned everything into metaphor, I felt those moles as interior creatures, as parts of me that remained in the dark, dependent on the me who could make it in the outer world, who could bring them food, meaning images and ideas. These they transformed into poems that they left in the twilight zone for the aboveground-me to retrieve, to haul out of the cave, to fashion and finish for the outside world. Without the twilight zone, what's aboveground and what's below would never meet. I'd have no poems, no shadows, no ladders or wells, none of this forward-looking, backward-looking uncertainty that plagues me now, waiting in this gray for the others to come.

Anthropologist Victor Turner describes the threshold in many cultures' rites of passage as a period of great ambiguity when the usual ways we define ourselves—our families, jobs, obsessions, personalities, ambitions—slough off. Major loss can do it: divorce, a rich midlife crisis, a loved one's death. But even after a new identity begins to build again, there's always the memory of the old one. Rilke says it this way: "This life that faces both ways / has marked the human face from within." Waiting here, I know that to the right lies the cave's stale air and darkness and to the left lies the passageway out, the light, the green, the song of indigo buntings. Such knowing marks us, stitches a shadow to even our happiest moments.

And maybe the twilight zone also unsettles because of the choice it embodies. And here's the real crux. Down here, thirty feet from the entrance well, in the gray-black overlap, in the presence of other creatures, some of whom come and go as they please, I too could easily turn around, go back up, tell Liz and the others I don't want to do it. There'd be sunshine at the bottom of the well. I could look up into blue sky and leafy overhang. I could figure out how to get back up that chimney, get in a car, stop for a bottle of wine, and go home. Being in the twilight zone means having a choice to go back or to go on. Nothing is forcing me one way or the other, not panic this time, not lack of equipment, not the pressure of others or ignorance of what lies beyond. I almost wish there were some force pressing on me, some real reason to compel my direction, someone to rescue farther in, a crucial phone call to get home for—any irresistible impetus to turn around or not. But there's only the quiet, the occasional muffled voices of Ron and Liz as she talks him down the chimney. Without my light on, there are only the barely visible shadows, the dank air. No reason to make either choice. Which makes it truly a choice. It's my call, a dilemma almost as scary as any situation in which love is a choice, not a necessity.

Another fear: In the twilight zone you can see, actually still *see*, what it is you're about to lose. You know that with a few more steps, the lumps and ledges of the cave walls will become invisible. There's an uneasiness about seeing the world grow dark in slow motion, an uneasiness that surprises me, who loves both dawn and dusk, who loves, especially, to sit in my home in the early evening with all the lights off and watch the day disappear, the slow diminishment of light, the way color drains from my couch and the edges of a table blur. Maybe that gradual darkening doesn't bother me at home because there I know that I can stop it with a flick of a light switch. Here, I'd have to move physically and I'd have to confess to others my fear. Instead, I walk carefully backwards, take another few steps deeper in, close to the farthest end of the twilight zone. I keep my hands touching the wall, as if I could keep something from slipping too far out of reach. This isn't a sudden loss of light, not its abrupt disappearance, as would happen in a three-second fall into a deep well or from a blow to the head, but a slow, eyes-open receding from one world, slipping into the next.

I've been watching Jeanne do it. Not in a cave, but on her living room couch. She'd been growing weaker and weaker, and on one particular afternoon, she seemed to have a foot in both worlds. Dressed in parrot green, her hair still short from the chemo, full of questions about my kids, my work, what I'd been reading lately, she seemed fainter to me, less substantial. As if her body had moved back a bit farther, even as it left her mind in the livelier light nearer the entrance, where she and I could still be together. Amid the difficult sadness, I was struck by the feeling she was still very present, but that somehow her very presence had many presences within it. I thought of the string of paper dolls I used to play with, how when you first cut them out, they lay as one doll, neatly compressed, a single silhouette until you began to unfold them, string them out across your lap. One of her was wholly present, talking with me, mostly about the small things that make up an intimacy between old friends, only occasionally about what it was like to die so consciously. I tried to name, silently, to myself, what seemed different about her.

She was thin, her shoulders knobby, her arms like sticks. But that wasn't it. It was true that she still looked outward and voiced her interest in my life, as if some part of her still faced the external world. But at the same time, it was as if all those other Jeannes, all of them still holding hands, had begun to unfold from her, to make a chain that reached across the present and into some other place, an inward place, perhaps, a place nobody else could see.

I suddenly felt as if her attention, the energy of her attention, was the same energy required when you try not to chimney down a vertical drop too fast. You push with your feet against one wall, your back against the other. If you let up the pressure too much, relax your body, you fall. If you keep the pressure even, slide one leg, a rump, one shoulder down at a time, you can control your drop, go down more gently. I wanted to throw her a rope, a seat harness, talk of a new treatment, summer plans, something, anything, to keep her from slipping farther or too fast. But Jeanne kept just enough of her gaze pushing outward while some other part of her was unfolding and pushing inward. It was as if for as long as she could maintain that pressure between inner and outer worlds, she could stay suspended here.

Every once in a while she'd close her eyes and I'd sit quietly, sure she was drifting off. And then suddenly she'd be back again, saying she hadn't been asleep at all, just drifting a bit. Where? I didn't want to know. She was a lifelong atheist who'd never believed in an afterlife, but wanted to know now if I thought she'd see her mother there. Amazingly, I had dreamed it, I told her, just a couple of nights ago, dreamed she'd been climbing a hill and I'd been behind her, and up over the crest from the other side came her mother whom I hadn't seen for thirty years, who'd been dead for fifteen. She smiled weakly. What else? she asked. Who else was there?

Ron and Rich have made it down the rope and into the twilight zone. I press myself against the jaggy wall and let them pass me. Rich knows this cave well and is eager to move in farther. I still want to linger where the light has not quite vanished. I sidle back and forth a few feet, watching the way the entrance light on my body deepens the green in my pants and then grays them, how my arms and legs grow less distinct the deeper in I go. A salamander, mottled mahogany brown and slimy, slips under a rock by my right foot.

It's missing its left front leg. Next to my shoulder sprouts a tiny tuft of pale green. Some seeds must have washed or floated or been carried in and found a small pinch of soil in the wall's pocking. It'd be a tough life, sending up a few shoots in the almost-dark, their stems leaning lightward. They look dwarfed and pale, a small forest of spindly-leafed, bent-over ghosts. Surely they're doomed; the organic material brought in from the outside, so crucial to cave creatures, is useless to them. Plants must have sunlight to survive and there's not much here. This spot, in fact, is probably the farthest reach of the plant world in this cave, the last remnant of green.

Beyond, the animals feed almost exclusively on death. And though aboveground there's the same eating of things smaller and less defensible, what strikes me as different is that up there carnivores chase, they hunt, they sniff out the homes of their prey. Vegetarians graze in the meadows, on tender forest-shoots. They trot and scurry and fly to food, to water, to whatever sustains them. Belowground, the cave creatures wait. Not for them the wild chase, the throat-slitting, the satisfaction of warm muscles in the mouth. Almost everything they eat is brought to them, delivered by others, deposited on the threshold. Most of it is already dead, maybe already decaying, broken down by bacteria into small bits.

In the twilight zone, you see what you're about to lose— whether it's sunlight, a friend, your own life—but because you can still see it, it's not yet gone and so you can comfort yourself, hang on a while. It's too soon to call in the paramedics, the change stoppers, not quite time to turn around. You take a few more steps, and still nothing sudden happens. Your monitors have to go on fine-tuning, trying to find the exact place where something crosses the line, where presence flips over into absence.

But here in the twilight zone, there is no such clear line.

Here things are both invisible and present; you're in the cave and not. The creatures around you wander back and forth: bats and pack rats, raccoons and spiders. Cerberus is here, and Janus, Hermes, all the other characters who mill around thresholds and gates, demanding their payments in wine or flowers, neither of which you've brought. You give away what you can: your desire to be clearly in one place or the other, your secret wish that that choice be removed, that someone else will tell you what to do, your private wanting not to see what you're about to lose. You hand them over, those secret wishes half-tainted with shame. You stand in the twilight zone in a gray world that insists on its uncertainties and paradoxes, on your status as mere stranger. Things get realigned, the psyche rearranged, a place for sadness enlarged, sureties and ambiguities put back in their proper balances. Jeanne is dying, a pile of scat blooms at my feet, a half-hidden salamander watches me from its cranny in the wall; Rich and Liz and Ron, now past me and well into the dark zone, call back. "You coming with us?" they want to know. "Or staying there?"

4

IMPURITIES

We leave a stain, we leave a trail, we leave our
imprint.... Nothing to do with disobedience.
Nothing to do with grace or salvation or
redemption.... It's why all the cleansing is
a joke.... What is the quest to purify, if not
more impurity?
                                    — PHILIP ROTH

SWIRLS OF REDS, blues, and golds sweep over Kubla Khan, a
fifty-eight-foot-high column of calcite, while music from
Adeimus' "Songs of Sanctuary" fills the Throne Room where
I'm sitting on a concrete bench. I can hear some of the others
next to me in the dark murmuring and sighing the sighs of
the satisfied. I know I'm supposed to be moved. And I am, a
little, but not by the musical light show, not even by the spec-
tacular formation bathed in one hymnal hue and then another. What moves me is all the effort in this cave, the millions of dollars and years of careful study that have been
expended in an effort to reduce the effect of us humans, who
are supposed to feel affected by what we see in front of us.

It would be almost comic if it weren't so deeply serious.

I'd first heard about Kartchner Caverns in southeast Arizona when the death of Randy Tufts and the story of the secret cave he and a friend had discovered made the obituaries of the April 2002 issue of the *New York Times*. The irony of a long-held secret enabling the eventual high-tech protection of the cave prompted me to book a flight to Tucson, Arizona, where I became one of the 180,000 people a year who descend into the caverns.

Minimizing the contaminating effect of visitors to Kartchner Caverns has been a top priority ever since 1974, when Randy Tufts and Gary Tenen poked around the cactus and dry brush of southeast Arizona and detected the unmistakable odor of bat guano. Its rank ammonia rose out of a small hole in the dry eastern flank of the Whetstone Mountains a few miles south of Benson. Experienced cavers, the two slipped down the hole and into an underground realm the size of two football fields. From the hundred-foot-high ceilings, thousands of formations dripped. They found no evidence that any human had ever been there.

Dumbstruck by the pristine beauty and almost burdened by the knowledge of its existence, the two men made a pact to keep the place secret until they could figure out how best to protect it. It's easy to imagine the logistics of their pact. If people ask where you've been, you say, "caving." If pressed, you name some nearby cave. Southeast Arizona is full of them. Beneath the land here lies a thick layer of Escabrosa limestone formed by ancient seas more than 320 million years ago. A series of faults opened fissures in the down-dropped blocks between mountain ranges. Water trickled in, widening and carving and dissolving the rock. Even when the climate warmed and the seas were replaced by deserts, the underground chambers remained, humid and dark, mostly unexplored. It was just such a cavern that Tufts and Tenen discovered less than thirty years ago.

For four years they regularly snuck into the cavern to map and photograph and marvel. Images of tourist-hordes beneath the tiny white helectites curling on the ceiling like bleached Chinese noodles must have haunted them; they told no one the cave existed, not even the owners of the property. They carried on with their ordinary, aboveground lives. But it seems inevitable that many things—cleaning the cellar, power outages, the sight of a bat, babies on their hands and knees, the smell of ammonia, waking up in the middle of the night in a dark house—would have reminded them of what they refused to disclose. Perhaps their secrecy even heightened the lure of what they could protect.

But what interests me is how one separates the aboveground life from the one below, and for once I mean that, not psychologically, but phenomenologically. How do you keep the actual stuff of one world from contaminating the other? I understand Tufts and Tenen's dilemma, their debating, even, whether to seal the entrance and keep the cave a secret, forever inaccessible. They must have known how seldom we humans can leave a thing alone, especially something with an aura of secrecy or the forbidden. A man once confided to me that some of the caves he took people to visit were "sacrificial caves," ones the local grotto, or caving club, agreed to guide strangers through in order to educate the public about cave ecosystems and the need for conservation. They accept that the price of such education is some deterioration of the cave. Humans are messy, he explained. They touch and litter; their residue gets strewn all over a cave. Knowing this, a local grotto may agree to guide you and other strangers into one particular cave and lie to you about all the others. "No," they'll say, looking you right in the eye, "this is the only cave around." Or the only one a novice can get into. Or the only one that's safe, not subject to ceiling collapse or unexpected flooding. They know that almost any human contact with a cave inevitably endangers it, that the only way to be sure we won't sully the subterranean pristine is to keep us out of it entirely.

After four years of exploring, Tenen and Tufts arranged a meeting with James Kartchner, a rancher, science teacher, and school administrator who had no idea that under the cactus and sand of his family's desert holdings, a world of bizarre beauty had been dripping, undisturbed, for millions of years. The circle of secrecy expanded. Tenen's wife was told. Then a few trusted cavers. They varied their hiking route to the sinkhole so that no trampled path would lead others to it. They even signed a document swearing themselves to secrecy, not just about the cave's location, but about its very existence. The penalty for exposing the secret, they threatened, would be divine punishment. When some other cavers happened upon the small entrance hole and made plans to widen it, a friend privy to the secret arranged for a few of the Kartchner brothers to gallop in, pistols brandished, and holler about private property.

For ten more years, the clandestine operations continued. The cavers went on mapping and photographing and, with the Kartchners, anguishing about how best to protect such a resource, finally deciding the best option was, paradoxically, protection through strictly controlled development. They went to see Bruce Babbitt, then governor of Arizona. Convincing him to put on a hardhat and overalls, they secretly led the governor up the mountain and slipped with him through the guano-reeking hole, along a narrow entrance passage, and into the caverns themselves. "Extraordinary," Babbitt reportedly said, and signed onto the project, promising full cooperation.

The intrigue continued. To avoid a media frenzy, the appropriations bill for Kartchner Caverns was deliberately buried in vague legislation about changes in accounting procedures. Until just before the vote, only six legislators actually knew that the bill authorized purchase of the caverns from the Kartchner family.

With Tufts and Tenen as consultants, the state made sure that only the most thoughtful design was approved, only the most advanced technology installed, and that all construction, all blasting and concrete-laying, wiring and plumbing were done with meticulous care. They erected mattress barriers to protect the formations from blast repercussions and hung giant plastic sheeting to keep moisture from escaping. The whole effort reminds me of operating rooms, the surgical gowns and scrubbing and sterilizing, the need to keep bacteria out of a messy wound—only in this case they were preparing for whole human bodies to descend into an incision they'd enlarged because what's inside is beautiful. Which it is—the world's longest soda straw—a thin, hollow stalactite—and this column in front of me without its gaudy lights, and in the previous passage, the walls draped in ancient calcite that resembles glistening medieval shields. Tenen and Tufts knew the cave would draw thousands of sightseers. And it does. Thirty years after its discovery and millions of dollars later, the cave opened to an expected 100,000 to 150,000 visitors the first year; it got 172,000. Now that figure is up to 180,000.

And all of us who visit Kartchner Caverns have hair and skin that the state of Arizona wishes to control. I'm not used to thinking about my body as a five-and-a-half-foot source of litter, but much of Kartchner's pioneering efforts have to do with containing what I and thousands of others unwittingly shed. Knowing this has made me aware of the woman seated next to me who keeps pulling a rubber band out of her ponytail, regathering her hair, and slipping the band on again. And of the skin on my forearms, always dry and needing to be scratched.

But it's actually lint from clothing that's one of the primary polluters in a cave. Cotton is one of the worst, the light fibers sloughing off my jeans every time my thighs brush each other, or every time I push or pull my hands into and out of my pockets. Dozens of small, almost-invisible threads of cotton and wool and thousands of skin and hair cells multiplied by hundreds of people a day, 365 days a year, and you can almost see the fuzz floating over the handrails, wafting down the passages, glomming onto wet soda straws, gunking up pristine cave pearls.

At Carlsbad Caverns in nearby New Mexico the problem got so bad that the staff instituted weeklong "Lint Camps," during which volunteers carefully pick lint from the trails system. In the last twelve years, they've removed 154 pounds of lint, that dry fluffy stuff you scrape periodically from the clothes dryer screen. One hundred fifty-four pounds of it. At Wind Cave in South Dakota, they even tried vacuuming each visitor before the person went underground. The problem with lint isn't just the unfortunate aesthetics of foreign matter on formations. It's also that lint seems to be a good source of organic material for various microbes that then produce an acid, which pits the fragile calcite.

Cave specialists all over the world are watching as the Kartchner staff works to control the hair and skin and lint that might gum up their cave. "How?" I asked Rick Toomey, the Cave Resources Manager for Arizona State Parks. His answer: mist and troughs and airlocks. It's the mist you notice first, a light shower almost. Even while you can still see the desert landscape behind you, you walk into a kind of carport that shelters the entrance to the cave. Ahead is a heavy door, similar to ones I've seen in maximum security prisons where they frisk you for contraband before you hear the metal thud behind you and the locks click back into place. It's a partially apt comparison. You've left your backpack in the Vistor's Center, along with the food and root beer prohibited inside the cave. You've been baking under the blaze of Arizona sun and suddenly you're in a mist you hadn't even seen. It's a very fine mist; it sprays your face, your clothes. You're dampened, not soaked. As the guide in his low voice explains the necessity of this ritual, my hair frizzes in response. Damp means less flyaway, fewer errant hair cells on the loose. Fewer clothing fibers, too. Just the bit of weight that water adds will help us keep our clothes on our bodies, every thread and fuzz-bit pressed by moisture back into our sweatshirts and jeans.

Moistened, we walked down a short passage. The guide waited until we'd gathered at the large metal door. When he opened it, we were ushered into a "conservation chamber." The door closed quickly behind us before the one ahead was opened. Someone behind me joked, "When God closes one door, he opens another." The doors reminded me not of God or opportunities but of hatches on submarines that a diver swims through and closes behind him, how he must wait until the water drains out to open another hatch and climb down to the main cabin. If the first one's not properly closed or if he opens the second one too soon, the ship floods, of course, and whatever's fragile—a human, for example— is quickly crushed by the pressure of the sea above.

It's not humans that the airlocks try to protect in Kartchner. It's speleothems, the array of intricate formations that have been growing here for millions of years. And it's not water the chambers try to keep out; it's desert air, which can ruin a cave. Outside, the humidity is about 6 to 7 percent. Inside the cave, it's 99 percent. You walk from arid to tropical in about four minutes. If you brought that aridity in with you, the ceilings would eventually stop glistening, the stalactites stop dripping, the helectites stop curling on the walls. The cave's fragile balance of seep, precipitate, and drip would cease; it would simply dry up. Colors would dull, the temperature rise, cave microbes vanish, the bats flee to cooler roosts. I've been in caves like that; "dead" caves, they call them. Still interesting, with convoluted passages, challenging squirms, and a few critters that call it home, but nothing's exchanged; in those places the cave's walls are dry, crumbly, no longer porous. I've felt more careless in such a cave, more likely to touch.

"The walkways, too," Rick Toomey had told me before I came inside, "are designed to reduce contamination." They're like gutters, I thought, leaving the Rotunda and heading for the Throne Room, giant, meandering gutters with flat bottoms and eighteen-inch-high curbs. "Another way to control the lint," he'd said. At the end of the day, a cleanup crew can hose down the walks, and the runoff is contained; it can't splash out. The curb also contains the walkway lights, which are dim and covered with gridwork. They come on only intermittently as we approach and turn off as we depart, another strategy to reduce the light and heat that can encourage the growth of algae, which can mar formations such as the bacon strip that hangs from the ceiling in the previous passage. These strips form when mineral bands of brown and gold alternate in a slab of calcite drapery. Because the slab is translucent, a carefully placed light behind one reveals what looks like a giant strip of fatty bacon. It's stunning and as subject to algae smudges as every other formation. In Kartchner, no permanent light highlights its colors, but next to it a pink ribbon is tied to the handrail.

I asked the guide to explain. "It's a marker for tonight's cleanup crew. Someone must have put a foot up on the curb here or touched the wall. They'll come through with a solution of bleach and wipe it down." Proud of the effort here, she added, "They wipe the handrails too, with a solution of bleach, every few days."

To keep the above world from contaminating the underworld seems an almost impossible job. The doors open and close at least seventy times a day. Thirteen thousand tons of human flesh pass through here every year. And once we're inside, misted and careful to keep our arms close to our bodies, sure not to litter in the cave, there's the problem of our breathing. Every time I exhale, I release carbon dioxide. So does the woman next to me. And the man at the front of the tour, the guides themselves, the cleanup crew, the hundreds of thousands of visitors who've been here since the secret was disclosed and the cave developed. Millions of carbon dioxide–releasing human breaths in five years in a fragile place that had known only the breathing of tiny bat lungs for thousands of years.

We could wear gas masks, I suppose, or they could install something that would siphon the poison out of the cave. But then there'd still be the problem of our being warm-blooded animals with a mean body temperature of 98.8 degrees. Already the temperature inside Kartchner has risen two degrees in some parts of the cave, and many think it's because of the heat radiated by so many human bodies. Unsure whether proximal bodies produce even more heat, I consider moving farther away from the ponytailed woman next to me but then begin to imagine the logical absurdity of what could be next: banning children with fevers and women with hot flashes, offering discounts to bald men and anyone dressed in polyester.

The Kartchner staff's control over how many people enter the cave each day and what we visitors do in here far surpasses that of most cave owners. The majority of wild caves in this country are on private land, and access is often unregulated. The result is countless acts of destruction—not just campfire-blackened ceilings and niches full of beer cans and pizza boxes, but serious defacement—graffiti spray-painted on cave walls, alcoves dug or chiseled into mud and stone. In numerous wild caves, I've seen formations broken off, whole sections of what look like amputated legs. The resulting problem isn't just an aesthetic one. The introduction of any foreign food—bread, oils, sugars—can change the dynamics of a nutrition-sparse environment. Suddenly there's a feast on the floor and all the rules for who eats what get suspended. What had been so delicately balanced can collapse into anarchy.

As Tufts and Tenen decided, the best prevention is better control over who from the outside world gets to go inside. The usual solution in a commercial cave is to limit the number of visitors and to make sure they're all accompanied by guides. The usual solution in a wild cave is to barricade the entrance. But then the dilemma is to design something that stops vandals but not everything else. Unimpeded airflow is crucial. So are the ingress and egress of small cave creatures, including bats. Some of the first gates constructed baffled the bats, many of which were forced to find other homes. Depending on the type of bat inhabiting the cave, horizontal bars of a gate must be a certain distance apart and angled just so. What a Virginia big-eared bat will fly through to get inside, a gray bat will not. Some species don't tolerate gates at all, some will tolerate one at the actual entrance, and others only if the gate is set farther back near the twilight zone. And once the gate is correctly designed, there's the problem of installing it, which, at one Idaho cave, required that thirty tons of angle iron, steel tubing, and floor and wall anchors be carried to the site and then into the fragile cave. In Virginia, a man has spent thirty years designing and installing hundreds of cave gates. Across the country, there are seminars on the design of bat-friendly gates. Workshops on gate installation. Debates on gate standards. Gate field tours. Internet journals by gate-building volunteers.

Organizations such as the American Cave Conservation Association do what they can to protect caves. They encourage people to "cave softly"; they lobby against the sale of cave formations, called speleothems; they remove graffiti with brushes and cover the abraded areas with color-matched mud. An organization in the Ozarks experiments with reattaching broken stalactites, using pins and bolts much as an orthopedist might repair a badly broken bone. In their widely circulated journal, the National Speleological Society used to publish articles about interesting wild caves and included directions to their entrances. But too many people — cavers, neighbors, and folks with too little to do — took up the invitation and descended into the holes, so many that the journal will no longer publish any directions at all.

Enormous effort, all of that, and none of it can be argued against by one who values conservation. Still, I wonder how far we're willing to go. It isn't just vandals in a wild cave that are hard to control. Or dry surface air in any cave, or lint, hair and skin cells, or the effects of body heat. It's also development of the land above the cave, which may be the most serious threat to what's below. Just clearing the land reduces the aboveground habitat for cave-visiting bats and rats whose feces, deposited underground, supply necessary organic material for the creatures that cannot leave the cave. In addition, new highways and airstrips increase the likelihood of gasoline, diesel, and oil contamination. New housing developments can affect groundwater supply and stormwater runoff; they can increase sediment deposition and pollute lime-stone areas with sewage. Redirecting runoff and drilling new wells can change the centuries-old supply of water that needs to seep into the cave to keep it alive.

Even if the troughs work, along with the misting systems and airlocks, even with the warnings about not touching, even if they control the migration of lint and keep people from littering and peeing in the caves, even if they can keep the desert air out of the cave and limit the impact of our hot and shaggy, breathing bodies, contamination is inevitable. How to know that and keep trying? How *not* to keep trying?

I'm reminded of the maitre d' at a fine restaurant who discreetly sniffs you when you walk in the door. He's hunting for perfume, hairspray, after-shave, anything fragrant that might contaminate the bouquet of the fine wines his customers order. There's something both comical and touching about the degree to which some will go to guarantee an exquisite experience that can't be guaranteed at all. What about onions? Someone's gardenia corsage? What about droughts, which some claim are causing Kartchner's rising temperatures? Or visitors in caves with runny noses and no hankie? And what about these lights on Kubla Khan? Somewhere in this room, they've secreted large spotlights and aimed the rainbow beams that pulse and fade with music piped in from elsewhere. It's as if without this spectacle—which, to me, merits as much anticontaminant attention as do our hair and skin—we wouldn't be convinced this cavern was worth all the meticulous attention given to keep it unpolluted.

I have great patience with the messiness of body, the unruliness of mind. I value them both as necessary parts of growing up, thinking through complexities, tolerating ambiguity, loving other people. Give me "the maximum amount of wildness the form can bear," as Donald Justice says about poems. I'd say it about places too. The world aboveground is roomy and resilient enough for a few tons of lint, the heat and detritus of our undampened bodies. Little need up there for misting showers and alert guides watching every hand-hold. But down here the world is fragile, barely balanced, unlikely to absorb loose ends, anything tattered. Tufts and Tenen were right to ensure that Kartchner be a carefully managed world. It's like a good zoo. Or certain churches. We've been baptized by mist, guided by a man who speaks in reverential tones, asked to sit on benches and contemplate a large formation that rises in front of us. "Songs of Sanctuary" fills the room. And yet if there's anything impelling here, it isn't in the sacredness of place or a sense of the otherworldly; it's the human ingenuity, the earnest effort not to muck up the pristine. And as with anything spiritual, there's the risk of going too far, of turning what might be moving, even inspiring, into something self-parodic.

Kartchner's not a dead cave. It's full of wet stalactites, calcite shields that glisten like blubbery parachutes, the first known cluster of needle quartz formations—tiny white pin-like clusters—in the country. The guide shines his light on certain features, but you can tell in the dim light that there are thousands more he's not highlighting. And they're still growing. An inch every hundred years. Water still seeps from above, the calcite keeps precipitating, the humidity, the monitors tell us, is stable. The cave is still alive and helped by another misting system installed discreetly inside it. You can't see the equipment, but you can see, here and there, a light spray, a drizzle from an invisible nozzle tucked beneath a rock. In front of me a young boy fidgets while just to my left a man watching Kubla Khan turn garnet and gold crosses his legs and absentmindedly strokes his beard. I don't know what they're thinking, but I could use a little less light on the subject.

5

MOONMILK

Each image changes, fuses with its contrary,
disengages itself, forms another image, and in
the end returns to the starting point.

— OCTAVIO PAZ

YOU'RE NOT SUPPOSED to touch moonmilk. It's fragile and
has taken years to grow to this large mass oozing down the
wall of an Oregon cave in the Siskiyous Mountains. It looks
like cream cheese, like an opaque-white, cave-dwelling jellyfish. What makes it so different from other formations, from
the cave itself, is its softness. Rock looms everywhere else,
stone, hardened calcite, boulders, and here's this gooey stuff
you could shape with your hands, mound up and smooth,
then place under your head like a pillow.

I'm inside a cave carved out of a gigantic block of marble.
I'm walking along marble passageways, marble under my
feet, above my head, marble chunks I step over, marble
rooms I enter and leave. This isn't polished, of course; it's
marble in its natural form, grayish white with a sugary tex-

ture that I can almost imagine cut into blocks and stacked into buildings, or sliced into small disks, coasters set beneath glasses of lemonade, images that vanish immediately when my elbow brushes against a jutting chunk. The ceiling hovers and the walls press, small clusters of gray-white chambers and crawlspaces where patches of moonmilk leak through the cracks.

You can't find moonmilk in eastern United States caves. Something about the temperatures, volume of seepage waters, and humidity have to combine in just the right way to allow its growth, a convergence that evidently doesn't happen in the East. But it's present in caves in the Italian Alps, in Australia, and in some western caves such as this one in Oregon. I've seen white inside a cave, of course, in calcite flowstones and stalagmites, in cave pearls and soda straws. But not this soft white, this shapeless mush of unknown origins. The ancient theory: When the moon's rays passed through rock and emerged into a cave, the rays took on substance, changed from light rays to white mass. Moonmilk, people believed, was embodied moonbeams. I like imagining why the rock of the moon would reflect sunlight while the rock of the cave would transform moonlight, what would make one a mirror and the other a shape-shifter.

Perhaps the difference has something to do with the cave as cocoon. In a cave or cocoon, you can't forget you've gone *inside* something the outside can't easily enter. You're cut off from the upper world, ensconced in the unlavished elsewhere, isolated, sealed away. You're protected from weather and hidden from predators; hidden, too, from mirrors and from others who can remind you who you are. Just the conditions conducive to change.

I think of the monarch caterpillar hanging upside down in its cocoon for fourteen days, safeguarded from marauders, the sun, rain. Inside its silky case, it doesn't have to think about hunger, a mate, where to find shelter. Protected, held, insulated, it does what it went inside to do. It changes; it rearranges itself, becomes something else.

And of a pearl, how inside the dark nook of an oyster shell it grows, layer after layer, thousands of layers of concentric spheres of calcite crystals known as aragonite, the same white mineral that leaks into caves and grows underground into flowerlike formations. The pearl grows undisturbed, a luster crystallized around a wound inside the darkness of the shell.

And of a black bear inside the dark cranny of her den, sleeping in hibernation while her own cubs emerge, wriggle to the nearest teat, settle in for weeks of sucking. They grow in the dark, even with their mother half-oblivious, while the cave shelters them from cold and others' hungers.

Pockets, sacs, recesses of protection and privacy. Pouches, pods, cocoons, chambers; think, even, of Clark Kent and his phone booth.

Vaults and crypts. What does the body's ultimate transformation require? That we minimize distractions so that our attention not be diverted from the monumental task at hand? Dark bedrooms, quiet hospice centers. Or that we orchestrate things so our minds stay stimulated, alive as long as possible? Rooms full of visitors, walls busy with photographs. Things lose substance, take on substance, change substance, and they often do so in enclosed environments that foster such change—the dark alcoves, the rooms so often small and sealed off like a hermetic chamber: cloisters and caves.

This cave began two hundred million years ago. There was no Pacific Ocean then, no Cascade Mountains, no rivers, nothing we could call a continent. There were rocks, a planet made of rocks. They lay in massive shields that shifted and ground, sometimes rose and fell. Two hundred twenty million years ago, in what we now call the Pacific Northwest, two massive rock formations began to angle toward each other, a stone creeping that probably took thousands of years of closer and closer until they finally sideswiped each other, the colliding edges buckling and folding, ripping open a massive depression into which water trickled and collected and deepened until the Pacific Ocean began to fill and small shelled creatures—mollusks, snails, scallops—began to evolve and die and drop to the bottom. The tiny bodies piled up and collapsed beneath the weight of the water, a whole layer of calcite-laden mud that hardened into limestone.

Thousands of years later the slow sideswiping turned more direct; the ocean basin rock—limestone—collided head-on with the continent. Rock melted, creating a massive molten mass that collided again with the limestone. And here's the most interesting change: When the molten rock got close to the limestone, the heat cooked it. Baked it. Turned it to marble that then rose and twisted and eroded, small cracks widening, leaving a labyrinth of down-sloping passages and small rooms.

That's what this cave is—one of the few marble caves in the country—small chambers of baked limestone that was once the compacted shells of sea creatures who once swam in an ocean that no longer exists. I think of the Taj Mahal, the marble monument to mourning that Shah Jahan built after his beloved died. I've stood inside that edifice, felt the way only such exquisite emptiness, such utter motionlessness on the banks of the River Yumuna, could ease the Shah's decades of grief. Its balm has something to do with the marble and light, how beauty can almost transform grief into stillness, make it possible for us to live with what's lost.

The guides in Agra like to place a flashlight against the

marble of the Taj Mahal, show tourists the way the stone becomes translucent, how it seems to glow from inside. The first time I saw that white glow, I thought of deep-sea divers, the way the light from their headlamps is soft, diffused by darkness. But there in the Taj Mahal, marble all around me, the tour guide shining his light through one section and then another, the light gets diffused by whiteness, everywhere around me a white ocean with tiny lamps, the struggle of Shah Jahan to lighten his grief, to lift it into domes and minarets in a way that I can't do, can't find any corollary to marble, white oceans, any antidote for the thickening sadness around me.

The rock in this cave is too thick to transmit any light except, as people used to think, for moonlight. Moonmilk is actually a cave deposit of calcite crystals and polycrystalline chains that accreted thousands of years ago in a process not unlike the making of most other cave formations. Moonmilk, however, has a high water content and some other ingredient that makes it oozy, and it's this ooziness that has mystified scientists for many years. Something organic? Someone touched the moonmilk inside an Australian cave eight years ago, left a handprint a centimeter deep, a handprint that has now disappeared, prompting speculation that the moonmilk had actually grown over the print, that moommilk is, in fact, organic, alive. On the cave wall in front of me, it looks now like an albino blob escaping from a hidden crack in the stone.

It's easy to imagine creatures lurking or crashing around in here. In many mythologies, the cave is the passage connecting Hades and the daily aboveground life. Literature and mythology are full of beings—Zeus, Hermes, even Jesus—brought into or taken from the world through a cave, bodies forming and dissolving in these subterranean rough marbled places. Here in this passage named Paradise Lost, stalagmites rise out of the marble floor and stalactites hang from marble ceilings. I peer into recessed alcoves, back behind half-walls, into the pocked up-above. Everywhere, small protrusions, hands, fingers, dismembered body parts. In the Ghost Room, more stubs, nubbins—relics, all of them, of larger formations that have been broken off or dissolved by acids, reminding me that it's often in caves that shamans of many cultures work their magic, singing over sickness and the future, changing their own shapes and the shapes of what floats in and out of their vision.

No ghosts, no monsters, no shamans here at all, of course. Knowing this doesn't stop me from remembering the time I watched a man in a cave change into a werewolf. It was my earliest memory of terror. I was much too young—maybe five or six—for such a movie. My mother had no idea what the show was about, that her twins shouldn't be sitting on either side of her watching the close-ups of a man's face as he turned into something else, his lips getting thicker, hair sprouting from his cheeks, his forehead, his flesh disappearing under a sudden mane of facial hair. It seemed like it took hours. I couldn't look away. Days later, at home in front of the bathroom mirror, I studied my own face, wondered if it could happen to anyone and what the first sign would be.

I think of Jonah.

Moving on down the passage, I leave the moonmilk and ghost images and enter a long, skinny room called the Whale's Belly. The stone seems to arch over and around; I'm walking down its throat and into its belly. I'm in a chamber that's inside a chamber. The rock looks rippled and then ribbed, grayish-white marble that's become bone and then gut. I imagine Jonah inside, the live chamber he rocked in for three days and nights in the darkness, weeds wrapped around his head as the whale dove and swam and rolled in the ocean. Whatever had made him flee from the task God had given him—fear? stubbornness?—he had three days to think about it, three nights to consider his death. Maybe sometimes it takes being locked in solitude, held away, isolated, in order to shift from defiance to gratitude. Or vice versa.

Or despair to resolve. My father was a POW in World War II. When I was thirteen, I wanted to know everything about his twenty-two months in Stalag Luft 3. I wanted descriptions of the camp, of the men, the way the guards treated them, what they ate for breakfast. My father was reluctant to talk about such details. "It was a long time ago," he'd tell me. I turned to books, especially to one called *Kriegie*. I made my father a character in the book so I could watch him move around the camp, thin, perhaps afraid, standing in lines for hours, forced to clean latrines and sleep on hard bunks. I imagined him miserable, a young man wrenched from his bride and having to endure cattle cars and meager rations.

Years later I realized what I'd wanted to know was how he'd gone from being that man to the man I knew—mostly cheerful, a big planner of projects, the president of the neighborhood civic association, a solid citizen, active member of the church—and whether that thin, imprisoned man was still inside him as he mowed the lawn and straightened his bow tie before work. Whether the postwar world, the demands of job and family had layered over his past like secretions over the irritant in an oyster or whether in the quiet of some too-long night, the long-buried past still pressed outward, sent him sailing alone on the Chesapeake with wartime despair, fragility, the patriotic rage not quite below the surface. "A lifetime ago," he'd remind me.

And I think of Kenny, one of my best friends, a practical, upbeat man who loves his wife and nuzzles his horses. Thirty years ago, as a sniper in Vietnam, he'd gotten hundreds of men in his rifle sights and pulled the trigger. I've spent countless hours with this man as each of us married others, raised our children, divorced, married others, countless hours over wine and Scotch and bowls of groundnut stew. I don't know that man in the jungle and I don't know how he went from one to the other. "A different me," he tells me, "from a different life, now over." Sometimes I watch him chopping wood, bending iron over the fire, and I try to see that other man inside him, the one I'm sure is still in there. And in my dad. Maybe in Jonah too, long after he'd gone on to years of praising God. No doubt inside us all are those other selves that we've silenced, perhaps for good reasons, or outgrown, or maybe partially transformed.

I think of pouches and eggs and of helmets, those cranium cradles, rounded shells of protection, how Hermes won't roam the underworld without one. On his head, it becomes one of the ultimate shape-shifters: It makes him invisible. In this altered shape he can travel back and forth between the worlds above and below. Underneath the helmet, the familiar winged feet, curly hair, and caduceus fade away, vanish, as he goes about delivering his messages, retrieving Persephone from the underworld, escorting Eurydice back to it. Hermes knows what happens in those regions, how to don a helmet and become something else, what orchestration of silence and invisibility it takes to get a message to the proper recipient.

I don't like helmets, don't like the way my hair gets smashed inside one, how my head feels a little wobbly with its weight. But I'd never go into a wild cave without one. Too many loose rocks, jutting walls, sharp corners, too many chances to split your skull open. It's the most crucial protection in a cave. If a cap in the underworld made Hermes invisible, a helmet in a cave seems merely to disguise the wearer; without telltale hair color or style, I have a hard time recognizing people underground. But like Hermes, too, a helmet allows the caver to squeeze into places no human should go. With your skull well protected, you feel freer to twist your head sideways, suck your chest in, contort your torso, squirm feet-first around a bend, become a shape less recognizably yours. I've been in wild caves with serene people who panicked, with aboveground bumblers who traversed a breakdown with the grace of Baryshnikov. Things happen to people down there. They become, on occasion, more or less than they were.

Or other than. A cave's cocoon-ness and its characters remind me we're probably all more loosely constructed than we can admit, that our selves are more truly, as Dr. Jekyll says, "trembling immateriality, the mist-like transience, of this seemingly so solid body in which we walk attired." Maybe it was that fear I felt the first time in a cave ten years ago when it seemed a Mack truck was bearing down on me, and I felt less firm than I'd thought, flimsy even, in the low-ceilinged chambers of ancient shape-shifting lore. I don't believe in literal cave monsters or vehicles barreling through tight passages and could not understand, could only feel, a sudden crowding. And now I wonder if that fear was some deeply embedded realization that I was crawling in a place that had, for many thousands of years, been the site of ancient shape-shifting. And maybe I was afraid of the transformation myself, not physical—not me into bats, vampires, bears, shamans, werewolves, Hyde—but me into other me's, the shifting of my own pasts and other selves, what's not quite disappeared inside, what lingers unseen, almost unheard. Perhaps I felt the embryonic flutter inside of another presence, and another, several, a whole congregation of fetal heartbeats beginning to stir, a myriad of other selves inside me awakened from deep slumber and beginning to stretch inside my body. "This human being is a guest house," Persian poet Rumi sings; "Every morning a new arrival." What I remember in that cave isn't song but fear and how heavy on my head my helmet seemed and how quickly, after I'd scrambled out of the entrance in a panic, I'd taken it off and dropped it. It rocked for a few seconds on the ground, rocked like a dark blue, broken-open, just-emptied eggshell.

This might be, then, the real sense of shape-shifting: not that anyone's face or body is permanently rearranged, but that here in the place where others can't see us, what's been hidden inside us might appear. The psyche might be reshuffled. Other, long-buried parts of ourselves might emerge. My father dropped bombs in the war, carried out secret missions, built cradles for his daughters' dolls, taught his son to sail. Kenny wiped out a hundred men, makes jewelry for his wife, loves to rest his cheek against a horse's muzzle.

A friend tells me a story about a man's transformation inside a cave. A brilliant, well-respected brain surgeon, the man stuttered so severely he could blurt out only a sentence or two before his tongue seized up, before his mouth locked into a series of misfired beginnings he couldn't speak his way out of. He'd practically given up talking and relied, instead, on writing notes to friends, colleagues, and patients. A friend who loved caving took him to a cave in France, a wild cave that they entered on their bellies, hunching themselves forward by haunches and elbows until they reached a deep subterranean room decorated with hundreds of stalactites hanging down, not quite touching the hundreds of stalagmites reaching up, none of the formations joined to form a solid column. It was a room full of one thing almost connecting to the other, and the surgeon gasped and blurted out, "It's so beautiful!" and then four or five more praises and then realized that for the first time in years he wasn't stuttering at all, a realization that launched him into hours and hours of fluency. Who knows what he said? The friend who told me the story didn't know and it didn't matter. What mattered was the cave and how, somehow, in its vault of incomplete columns, the man's syllables connected in one graceful sentence after another. When it was time to go, they retraced their steps and belly-crawls and reemerged into the sunshine where the stutter, though reduced, resumed. The man repeated the experience again and again, squirmed into the cave the way others might check into rehab, took his cure underground among the disconnected stones.

Inside this Oregon cave, moonmilk oozes down another marble wall. There are no reflective surfaces in these passages, not even enough pooled water to look into. The cave is full of fossils, is, itself, carved out of the graveyard of ancient shells that became limestone and then marble, which Shah Jahan used to transform his grief into beauty. I want to remember this, how the belowground world might give rise to change—shape, emotion, psyche. I can't see much of anything in the dim light; anything, anyone, is possible. Mother Theresa once said she knew she had a little bit of a Hitler inside her. And I, most likely, a bit of a Hyde.

Moonlight to moonmilk, human to ghost, vampire to bat —prime cave-dweller which, the Kanarese people of India say, is itself the product of a failed transformation. They believe that bats were once birds that wanted badly to be changed into humans. In their bat form, they entered the temple chamber to pray for such a change, and the gods, in their perversity, decided to grant them a little of what they wished for and changed them from bird to mammal. They substituted a snub nose for a beak, moved their eyes to the front of their faces, gave them a pair of breast nipples for suckling their young, removed the feathers and gave them hair instead, and finally put some teeth in their mouths. I'd like to have witnessed the story-making, seen how the Kanarese studied birds and bats and imagined bird eyes migrating to the front, feathers losing their silk, becoming whiskery. I'd like to have been there when mystery turned into story, when the unknown took on a different shape. But, no, the gods evidently decided, no witnessing by humans, and no substituting hands for wings and no upright posture. And for comedic effect: big ears. What emerged from the temple was a creature halfway between bird and beast, so ashamed of its appearance it fled to the caves and emerges only at night.

There are bats in this cave, Townsend's big-eared bats and Pallid bats, some of which live record-long lives here, up to twenty-six years. But no vampire bats, which, it turns out, don't suck blood at all. They lap it up, like a dog at its water dish. A small bite on the skin of a cow, a pig, sometimes horses or birds, and the bat settles down at the edge of the wound and leans over, its small tongue flicking the blood into its mouth, its presence a barely noticeable flutter on the neck.

Here in Oregon Cave, I'm glad today for the lights, room to walk upright, more moonmilk on the wall. In spite of the taboo against touching, I touch it. It's soft; it yields; I can press my finger into it. Its name comes from the German word *mannlimilch*, meaning "little earth-man"; gnomes, in other words, who supposedly delivered the white mush from the netherworlds and left it in caves for humans to use. Which they did. Whether people believed moonmilk was reflected moonlight transformed into substance or a gift from the gnomes of the underworld, they believed in its curative powers and used to spread it, like cream cheese, on livestock wounds. Like magic, it cured infections, speeded healing, acted as a balm for wounds.

Scientists suspect now that the stuff is home to a certain microbe, *Macromonas bipunctata*, the same type of bacteria used in modern antibiotics like Neosporin. But the mythologies haunt: this cave, this chamber of shape-shifting, of image disengaging, reforming, harbors a mysterious substance, maybe a gnome-gift or reflected moonlight that's taken on form. And whatever its origin, here's what it does: It closes the wound.

THE SOLACE OF BEAUTY

The love of form is a love of endings.

— LOUISE GLÜCK

"CAVE ROT," he calls them, pointing to the fantasia of shapes —stalactites, cave pearls, clusters of calcite grapes—that have seeped from these cavern walls for thousands of years. My guide Mike and I are knee-deep in an underground stream in a skinny cave in upstate New York. To him, the speleothems in this narrow, winding passage are just crusty structures that form when the mineral-laden water oozes into the interior of a cave and then evaporates, leaving behind a calcite deposit. A mostly chemical reaction that indicates, he says, a cave with wounded, leaky skin. He likes his caves less adorned, less vulnerable to human mutilation. I see his point immediately when my foot slides off an underwater rock and I lurch to the right, grab a small protrusion on the wall. It doesn't break off in my hand, but enough oils from my skin, the skin of everybody else who's slipped on this same rock, will eventually turn this small, ancient knob black. It's inevitable, I suppose, that such protrusions become irresistible to klutzes and fondlers alike. I'm a little of each, and if I don't stay better balanced and more restrained, I'll add my own layer of stain to the cave.

If Mike's annoyed with my clumsiness, he doesn't show it. Sloshing ahead of me, he swings his headlamp widely— up to the ceiling and down to the water, down the long passageways—in a way that makes me think he's more interested in the joints and fractures of the passage itself and its level of water than in the formations that grow here. I run one finger lightly over a small stalagmite. It's surprisingly smooth, almost glazed. I resist Mike's calling it cave rot; these seeping leaks from the cave's wall are to me oddly appealing. I know they've grown here by having oozed through something else and been left behind on the wall as a precipitate. I even know a bit of the mineralogy—that when a solution rich in dissolved carbon dioxide enters the low carbon dioxide atmosphere of the cave, the solution will equilibrate, causing its carbon dioxide to vanish into the cave air and leaving the calcite precipitate behind to grow visible on a cave wall.

"They have a trigonal crystal system," Mike says. He's waded back to me to explain something about the shape of the minerals that make up the formations. But I'm drawn to color and texture, the swirls and drizzles of ivory and raw umber, of henna sand and gold. The glazed and polished, the pocked and nubbly. And decorations, the baroque and rococo, the beading and scrollheads, the finials and friezes. This is just the kind of belowground extravagance to balance my aboveground reserve.

And this is just the kind of ornamented praise that makes Mike roll his eyes. Though I've stayed completely silent, he seems to know what I've been thinking and goes ahead again, leaving me in the mostly-dark, which becomes the oddly-dark when I start flicking my headlamp off and on. Shapes loom and disappear. Patches of color swing in and out of the light beam. Coherence breaks down; I'm in a room with an erratic strobe light on my head. Nothing, neither the formations nor their allure, makes any sense; but neither, perhaps, does beauty, which is not, for me, an intelligent response to something, but a kinetic one. Beauty pulls us toward it. In the presence of something beautiful, a burnished stalagmite, for example, a white lily, or a man, my initial response of aesthetic pleasure will, most likely, become emotional pleasure, which rouses all the senses that propel me toward whatever it is that appeals. I'm not much interested in the aloof beauty of a formal garden or carefully styled hair on a man. The poet William Matthews says, "Aesthetic distance is usually about feeling superior to emotional life and contains a built-in reason for not asking why." I'm after the opposite, what he calls aesthetic intimacy. Isn't beauty something to go toward? In this case, I want it up close, in my hands. I want to enter it; I want its play of shadow and light. I rub my hand lightly over a slightly blackened stalactite suspended above my head and realize I'm even drawn to the faint stain dozens of other hands have left behind.

Somewhere up ahead, Mike's sloshing has stopped. Except for the water, the cave is silent. I swing my head in small circles, using my headlamp to scan the passage ahead. Nobody there. The water gushes past my knees. It's turbid, sediment-stirred, meaning Mike's feet can't be too far ahead. And where would he go, anyway? This cave, Mike said, is a single winding passage. It ranges from three to maybe eight feet across, about twenty feet high. It burrows like a sinuous crypt back into the mountain about a half-mile. Depending on how the aboveground streams drain in a downpour, this wouldn't be a good place to be in a storm. My mind goes to the Swiss cavers caught not long ago in a flooded cave, how they had to scramble up the interior walls as the water rose, how they held onto tiny ledges for seventy-two hours until rescuers arrived. Deep in a cave, you have no idea what's going on above ground, whether it's night or day, whether the sun's still shining in 90-degree heat, or whether clouds have moved in, thickened, become ominous, whether there's been a fierce downpour up there, the rivulets suddenly full and gushing into channels that dump into this stream that becomes a river, the water rising, rushing down the chute toward you. For a moment, the vision of my cousin's death returns, the truck barreling down the highway in his side-view mirror, and I speed up, wanting to find Mike, my hands grabbing anything to steady me. Then suddenly, around the bend, he's waiting for me.

He nods his head toward a small alcove. Despite his disdain for the formations, he shows me a half-dozen cave shields, each the shape of a large plate, oozing from the wall. They're a flotilla of jellyfish, I decide, caught off course, petrified into stone. Another formation, three feet up on the left wall, looks like a cluster of marble grapes, a little past their prime. Their skins wrinkle a bit but you can see in them their former luster, their history of polish and shine. Or maybe they're eggs, some gooey with mucous, some gone to stone. I lean my head back and shine my headlamp higher up. There's an ocher-colored cone, the curious yellow-brown of scorched prairie, plucked from a Midwest drought, rolled into a funnel and hung in the cool darkness of a cave. It glistens; a single drop clings to the tip. Beyond it hangs a cluster of soda straws, buff-yellow and hollow, an orchestra of tiny recorders, their mouthpieces embedded in stone, a single drip suspended from every end, each one a note of some subcelestial music—a requiem? An elegy? Mike ducks his head under a heavy woman's leg that's been whittled to a point. A solitary drop dangles from the leg.

A stalactite like this grows very, very slowly: about a half cubic inch, the size of your thumbnail, every fifty years. Within that time span, major wars are fought, countries realigned, whole lives lived. In that time span, my friend Jeanne has traveled the world, risen to the top of her profession, created a community of friends that matter, been my lifelong confidante and memory-sharer, battled cancer, won, lost, battled and battled and battled and now is dying way too young, and all the while this stalactite has grown another half inch. It's now about eighteen inches long. *Patience,* I used to try to tell Jeanne, waiting for the chemo to shrink the tumors. I had no idea what I was saying. I take my flashlight from my pack, wade closer, and put the end of it smack against the slab. The light enters the stone, shines through. It takes on the look of lit marble, a soft white glow in the dark. It looks alive.

When we were little, my brother and sister and I used to close the curtains in the living room, turn off the lights, and kneel on the couch to face the large mirror that hung on the wall behind it. My brother would do it first: put the end of his flashlight in his mouth and turn the switch on. His puffed-out cheeks glowed reddish-orange, a couple of small, skinned melons lit from inside. We'd stare and stare, his eyes receding in the dark, his face almost unrecognizable. This was the boy who'd jump out of closets, hide under beds, scratch the inside of closet doors, whose greatest delight was frightening his younger sisters. And there he was in the mirror, his cheeks shining, blown up with light. We knelt there, mesmerized on that edge between creeped out and thrilled. And then we'd do it too, my twin and I, opening our mouths as wide as we could, wiggling the light in, pulling a bit of cheek out and over the edge, sealing the leaks between lips and flashlight. And then we'd force air into our cheeks and push the switches on and watch ourselves become something else, three pairs of bulbous cheeks glowing where our faces should have been. The unspoken agreement was to freeze for a few moments in this position. We'd stare at ourselves, at one another, our flashlights like giant corks in our mouths and then, together, we'd begin to deflate, inflate our cheeks. Everything recognizable disappeared. What remained in the mirror was a rhythmic pulsing of lit, stretched skin, three double-lobed sacs beating in the dark, each with a small blaze way back in the throat, radiating red-orange and peach, red-orange and peach, the mouth like a dangerous opening, plugged to keep the fire inside until the sight became oddly familiar and we'd finally unplug our mouths, drop our flashlights, raid the fridge for peanut butter and jelly.

The body offers other experiments in permeability: the way I can push a sewing needle in and out of the tip my finger without drawing blood. Pierced ears. Even hand lotion that sinks in, dramamine patches, tattoos. And years later, nicotine patches and birth control patches, drugs seeping right through our skin, all evidence that skin isn't impervious, that things can pass through it, and through bone, too. Months after I'd badly broken my tibia, I watched the surgeon remove a six-inch steel pin that had been inserted perpendicular to the bone at the time of the accident and left with its ends sticking out a half inch on either side of my leg a few inches below my right knee. I watched him grab one of the protruding ends and pull. I could see the other end disappear into my leg, feel an odd pulling, something sliding through the inside of my leg, watch the end he held onto grow longer and longer until the entire pin emerged from a body more pervious than I'd thought.

I'm struck by how the cave reveals the world as gradations of permeability. This calcite can drip and grow in the dark because one of a cave's peculiar qualities is that it, too, is permeable. This hollowed-out chasm must have been a seam of very porous limestone, susceptible to rapid dissolution that allows me now to walk inside it. The remaining walls are porous enough to let moisture seep through and minerals to grow. And it isn't just water that penetrates: this calcite, which isn't porous, allows light to pass through, making it look alive with luminescence.

Because aesthetic intimacy insists on asking why, it requires a certain openness in the observer. I know its opposite, when I've felt encased and armored, steely with jealousies and insecurities, felt anger like a metal shield. I would have been miserable here then, brittle disdain making me impervious to the cave's pleasures. How much do we block out, resist, deflect? How much skids off us because it cannot get inside us? So many things don't interest us because we cannot find a way to let them in.

I take the flashlight off the calcite flowstone. The circle of light disappears, the slab becomes a slab again, pale, pearly, but not lit. Meanwhile, up on the beaches of South Jersey, you pick up an emptied conch shell. The animal it housed is long dead; all that remains is a skim of sand inside. You press it to your ear and you swear that way back in there, at the far end of the spiraling sheen, the waves and the surf of the sea are still there. In another million years, the minerals of this shell may leak from an undiscovered cave wall. Some human may someday find it in another form, a stalagmite growing in the dark.

The opposite might also be true: Lock out water and light

completely, and a substance remains closed, opaque, unyielding. Rubber doesn't grow translucent, bronze resists erosion, clay pots persist as shards. And we humans have our ways of preventing intimacy. We bang our pots, our shields, our chests, while we long for what we shut out. Admit water and light inside a substance and it opens, becomes transparent, transformed. Limestone becomes a cavern, soil yields, calcite glows. The analogy appeals, but I can hear Mike now: *It isn't a matter of science for us. The cave's a place, not a human being.*

I have a geode from out west, a lava bubble that hardened and emptied. For centuries it lay buried in the earth, indistinguishable from layers and layers of lava and sediment that surrounded and piled up on top of it. Meanwhile, into its cavity a little water dribbled and then left, and then a little more, and something grew in its dark recess for thousands of years until someone picked it up and sold it to the tourist shop where I stood one day, picking up one or another for ten minutes, trying to guess from its heft what lay inside. What did I want? A mostly hollow geode, plenty of space, and long crystals? Or a dense interior, the minerals compacted? The woman next to me, also trying to decide what she wanted, finally chose one, which the clerk cut open with a diamond saw. He held it out to her, one half in each hand, the newly exposed interiors belly-up. She gasped. Not a hollow spot inside. Instead, a smooth, cross-sectioned world of white swaths and undulating lines. It looked like a varnished sand painting of chalky dunes and hazel horizons. You could almost imagine the thinner, darker lines as hieroglyphics written on polished marble, a message encrypted some thousand years ago. The woman was pleased, liking, I assumed, her treasures full and glossy. She decided to wait with me, to

see if I would be as lucky. I bounced one geode and then another in my hand, trying to guess what the heaviness meant,
what a thin crust might suggest, whether to go with the
biggest. In the end I just picked one and the clerk cut it open.
One half looked like a conglomeration of petrified snow and
mud, a bit of clay, something that had been smashed beneath
a truck tire and turned to stone. The other half was raggedly
pocked. The woman clucked in disappointment, maybe
sympathy, and left, clutching her prize. Back in the motel
room, I turned the geode this way and that under a lamp and
could see the pocked side had several small crannies, a tiny
cave system locked inside a rock the size of an orange. The
passages connected beneath the medial bridge of stone. The
passage on the left had a smaller opening the shape of a
cockeyed figure eight, but under a bright light I saw how it
opened up toward the back of the rock. Farther in, the interior was speckled with white crystals, a pocket full of
minarets and pearls and glassy jewels that sparkled in the
beam of my flashlight. I loved its initial appearance of disar-
ray, its messy, shoved-together stripes and arcs and lumps of
mismatched material, gray stipples and streaks on the few
flat surfaces, and that its beauty grew from the tension
between compression and bubble, between crowding and
space.

Mike returns and describes what's ahead: The passage bends
to the left about thirty feet ahead, then twists to the right and
narrows, and in one short section, the walls angle in near the
top. You feel, he says, as if you're walking beneath an A-
framed roof made of stone. There are no squeezes ahead, but
an odd jumble of rocks at a bend. I picture a knuckle inside
the dark finger of the cave, which twists and burrows. He's
getting animated and I want him to keep talking. "Each inte-

rior has its own identity," he tells me, "its own configuration. It's long and windy or stubby and bouldered. It has sudden drops or gradual inclines. The walls are close or they're not." He describes one cave's pit entrance, another's confusing side passages, the way one cave feels like a high-domed cathedral, another a rabbit warren, how one has arms that twist underground like a Medusa made of emptied space.

People leave, they change their minds, they die, beloved dogs die, children grow up and move away, you give up one more myth, the body sags and fails. Finally, even the illusion of immortality evaporates, leaves behind, at most, our small protestations: words, a few notes, a brushstroke, some oil-stained chunks of marble that, if they're porous enough, perhaps we can polish and shape, fashion into art. Into, as Robert Frost says, "a momentary stay against confusion." But the truth is, the cave's hollowing-out began millions of years before its formations began to grow. And since it's impossible to slow down time for the cavern's erosion or to speed up time for the stalactites' growth, there's no hope of catching up. Again I think of Jeanne dying during the summer of 2001. As in the cave, I know what's being emptied grows faster than what can possibly fill it, which may be why Mike's drawn to the contours—though he'd never say so—of the void itself, its passageways, and not its stalactites, which—and this he does say—are too easily broken, too stained by touch.

We turn around, head back downstream. If I've learned anything from him in this cave, it is that I ought to add architecture to my aesthetics, some appreciation for the shape of the space itself. And that I ought to suspect that wanting my hands on the glistening growths of calcite is a wish that the cave could do what ultimately no religion can do either: insist that the solace of forms can fend off the void. It can't. Perhaps only art, beauty, can, and only for a while. In spite of whatever mockery of his I might invite, I do it again: run my gloveless hands over flowstone and stalactites. Mike's in front of me noting water levels, both of us headed for the brightening light and the cave's wide open mouth.

ELEPHANTA CAVE AND
THE EROS OF MYSTERY

... the great interests of man: air and light, the joy of having a body, the voluptuousness of looking.
— MARIO ROSSI

There is no Paradise, no place of true completion, that does not include within its walls the unknown.
— JANE HIRSHFIELD

CHITRA WEARS no helmet, no headlamp, no boots or mud-caked overalls. The boat we've just stepped from isn't a canoe we paddled to a remote upstream ravine and the cave we're headed for isn't a secluded one tucked into canyon walls, unpeopled and silent but for the drips. We're on an island an hour outside of Bombay; hundreds of people mill around under the hot Indian sun. Her dark hair pulled back in a bun, her feet in simple sandals, Chitra, the guide I've hired for this visit, glides effortlessly through the crowds and the pesky monkeys, the souvenir stalls crammed with postcards and marigolds. Her bright green sari flutters in the breeze as we pass the palanquin bearers and head up the steep stairway toward the cave.

Partway up, some combination of jet lag and sun and so many bodies, so many languages, and the sickeningly sweet smell of blossoms on the overhanging trees all begin to press too close. I pause on the stairs and close my eyes, trying to shut it all out for a moment. "Come," Chitra says, right beside me, "you'll feel better inside the cave." A group of turbaned men and draped women flows up the stairs from behind, parts to go around us, melts back together and continues up. "Come," she says again, and I'm reminded of the time a colleague from India led me up a narrow flight of stairs to show me her bedroom in Maryland. She kept the heavy window curtains drawn, and next to her bed stood a small altar. I remember it draped with luxurious cloths, a swirl of fuchsia and lime, and adorned with beads, crowded with small bowls, maybe incense burners, bright photos of blue Hindu gods and black Kali. Some sort of small light on the altar made everything glow, made the colors deepen and shimmer. She treasured her gathered icons, felt peaceful in their presence. I wondered then, as I do now, whether such richness would keep me awake all night or cause me to shut my eyes just to escape it all.

I open my eyes and continue the climb. At the top, outside the cave entrance, children crowd us, offering to pose for photos in exchange for a handful of rupees. I walk quickly on, shaking my head no, which doesn't deter them. In front of me, they skip backwards, smiling, "photo? photo?" or they run alongside me, "photo? photo?" until Chitra steers me to the left at last and into the entrance.

Elephanta Cave was carved out of the solid basalt of the island's mountain more than fifteen hundred years ago by unknown artists who experimented with freestanding sculptures and figures three times the size of human beings. The cave mouth itself looks as if it's propped open by a series of massive pillars, as if only they keep the flat, rough stone of the ceiling and the mountain above it from collapsing on our heads. It's an illusion, of course, one of several in this country, in this cave, maybe in all caves, that disorients me, leaves me feeling as if I can't quite say what I'm seeing.

The temple is laid out symmetrically, a geometric mandala that's meant to spin energy inward and outward. It replicates the cave high in the Himalayas that is supposed to be Shiva's permanent residence, and indeed there's a strong feeling here of having been transported to another world. The figures are all huge; even the dwarfs that guard the doorways lower over me. They're oblivious to the thousands of people, devotees and tourists, who come to the cave, and they hint of ancient secrets we can't penetrate. They seem to stare at each other and the cave floor. We're invisible here, trivial and unnoticed among the old dramas they enact: passion, revenge, duty, and play.

Maybe because I'm still feeling woozy, unsettled, and crowded, I stay in the outer chambers where I can keep my eye on the sea while I get used to the cave's cooler air. Here, too, though, people press and mingle and whisper as light from the three side entrances pours in the openings, bends around pillars, seeps into the alcoves and outer rooms, shifts, shadows one carving and illuminates another. Chitra's stories enliven them all: the voluptuous carvings of Parvati and sculptures of Shiva, panels of Shiva loving Parvati, Shiva pinning Ravana beneath a mountain, Shiva gambling and quarreling and practicing yoga, calming his lover and impaling demons. Shiva is the Hindu god of both destruction and procreation, and the outer rooms at Elephanta Cave practically shimmer with all his forms, his loves and rivalries, tricks and devotion, deaths, births, his earlobes and elbows, hair, bracelets, all of it detailed in stone, all of it reminding me of the streets I just left in Bombay, the crush of flower baskets and beggars, the mix of mirrored temples and shanties, the too-packed boat ride and long climb up to the cave. I close my eyes, try to shut it all out again, but the smells take me back to where I'd been a few days ago, in the temple at Nathdwara.

The doors there open only a few times a day. Hordes of pilgrims mass outside, waiting. At 4:30 that afternoon, I took off my shoes, felt the cool marble underfoot as the jostling grew more frenetic, and when the doors finally opened, the mass swooped inside and carried me along. It seemed that I could've moved without my feet ever touching the floor, the bodies were that close. A surging ferry of silk and flesh swept me into the temple and paused only briefly at the entrance to the inner sanctum where a Vishnu icon, a black stone, sat in a recess so far back I could barely see it. The women around me seemed to know what they were looking at. They paused briefly in front of it, tossing flowers and rice, muttering, elbowing me out of their way, shoving against my back when I stood too long, straining to see what drew them here with such fierce devotion—something back in that unlit alcove of plain walls which they paid homage to and I could barely glimpse before they surged on, before I was swept along again, around a corner and back out into the courtyard. What was it, back there in its private recess? What was it I couldn't see?

Though Chitra talks quietly, her musical voice rising and falling as she ushers me from one underground room to another, India's cow-jangling crush of beauty and filth has made me jumpy, has made me eye the shadows these stone figures, frenetic too, cast on the damp stone walls of the cave, as if here, too, I can't be sure of what I'm seeing. In one of the stone panels, Parvati and Shiva are naked from the waist up. Her breasts are almost as large as her head; his chest is firm. If their arms hadn't been broken off by marauding Portuguese in the sixteenth century, they'd be touching each other, maybe holding hands. Locked in this pose for over fifteen centuries, they remind me of the lovers on John Keats's Grecian urn and his consolation to them: "Do not grieve; / She cannot fade, though thou hast not thy bliss, / Forever wilt thou love, and she be fair!" As on the urn, here in the cave the ceremony never ends, they never turn to each other, lie down on the stone floor, never consummate their marriage.

Along the passages, Chitra shows me the dwarf and starts another story. I half-listen, but mostly I become aware he's minus part of his lip. And here's a doorkeeper whose front half below the waist has been sheared off. In the Gambling Scene, Shiva has no arms, and the flying figures above him are missing most of their kneecaps. And here, Shiva dancing, his legs broken off, and there, in the Lord of Yogis panel, the arms are missing. In others, the nose is gone, bellies cracked open, feet missing, a face, a breast, a shoulder. Their damaged bodies crowd the cave walls, and they go on anyway, striking the poses and enacting old dramas.

Outside, clouds must be skitting across the sun: In here, the light shifts again. The figures are almost freestanding yet seem bound to the rock from which they emerge. In the largest panels, figures appear to form small groups—Parvati with Himalaya, who's also her father, and then, from another angle, no, Parvati's with Shiva. Or is Shiva alone? Or are they a threesome? Or is Himalaya really consorting with the fan bearer or the fan bearer with Candra? They all seem shifting, sliding imperceptibly toward and away from one another while light and shadows keep the whole panoply in flux until finally I have to turn away.

Chitra at last leads me past the frenzied carvings, up a few steps, between the giant stone doorkeepers, and into the darker recess of inner sanctum, the spiritual center, she says, of the entire cave. The walls are plain, unadorned, flat slabs of stone on all sides. It's a relief, this lack of ornament, this sparseness in the middle of such intricacy. I finally feel permission to pause, am able to rest my eyes without closing them. The room is almost empty except for the low platform from which rises the phallus of Shiva, erect, thick, waist-high. Even here, shadows play on it. One moment, it's polished and dark; the next, taut and tan, and then veined, stippled. It suggests both a massive erotic force rising out of its rock platform and a poised but motionless energy. The stone floor around it is strewn with coins and the small, smoldering offerings of incense. A lone devotee stands in front of it, a bone-thin, gray-haired woman wrapped in a yellow silk sari. Her cupped hands are full of flowers; her face is unreadable. In bare feet, she climbs up onto the platform as her sari slips slightly off one shoulder.

My hands are empty, but even if they weren't, I wouldn't know what to do. Or why I'd do it. I watch the woman on the platform bow before Shiva's phallus and I wonder if she can say why she does what she does, whether her worship is wordless, needs only her gestures and offerings. She extends her flower-laden hands and drapes a garland of marigolds over the phallus's smooth, rounded top. Oblivious to or perhaps ignoring my curiosity, she keeps her eyes on the phallus, steps back and stands still, palms pressed together.

I keep my eyes on it too. What am I trying to see? I know what a penis looks like. I've seen a number of them in various states, even adorned a few myself. But this one doesn't suggest fun or sex, not even the simple warmth of another, makes, in fact, those pleasures seem merely human by comparison.

The phallus is known in India as the lingam, and stories about the origins of its worship are as numerous as the Shiva-arms in this cave. According to one of them, when Shiva and Pavrati were making love one afternoon, he had positioned a bull at the doorway to prevent any interruptions. When the Brahmin Bhrigu came to visit and found his entrance blocked by the bull, he cursed Shiva, declaring that henceforth he be worshipped as a phallus, or lingam, since sex was what had so occupied his attention that he could not even get up and greet a Brahmin.

I imagine that any number of men might find this not a curse, but a worthy fate. Consider the message: A man decides that making love to his beloved is more important than receiving an unannounced visitor, who then promptly punishes the man by declaring that his penis shall forever more be worshipped by both men and women. They'll bow down to it, bedeck it with flowers, circumambulate it, erect little shrines all over the countryside. Phallus worship, born of passion and closed doors.

Raised in the West and wary of praising too much testosterone, I don't know how to think about such devotion. I don't know how to make the phallus more than it is, though I know it seems more than physically large here. It's a symbol, Chitra reminds me, of destruction and procreation, of power and mystery.

I'd long ago sensed in my father the power of a secret. Pressed during a conversation once, he refused to answer my brother's questions about a certain part of his past, saying he had secrets he'd take to his grave. Which he did. None of us ever knew them. Something about the war? His clandestine operations in a POW camp? About his marriage to our mother? Other women? Whatever his secrets were, he wasn't crippled by them, had no need to tell, no wish to reveal them in hopes of greater intimacy or deeper understanding. His silence about them was not, I think, the result of shyness or shame, but reserve, something held back, preserved for or from another time and place, protected even, and therefore valuable. *What?* I sometimes wanted to ask him and never did.

What? I want to ask Jeanne. *What's back there?* And to Chitra and these many Shivas: *What would you say to us, to me? What do I need to know?* The figures dance and love and play and destroy, but they never answer. They remind me that good stories, like bodies, are penetrable only up to a point, probably not knowable. And that in entering them, the possibilities of intimacy—and its opposite—deepen. I know that when lovers tell each other secrets they often feel their bond grow stronger, and I know that withheld secrets can cause distance and distrust. But I also know that the best of intimates understand the other has left some things unsaid, and they learn to trust not knowing it all. I value an intimacy that's incomplete and therefore hopeful. Eros for me has often been about what's missing or concealed. It is that which I yearn toward. Or slowly reveal. To keep a secret is to make a pact with one's interior, which grows larger because of what's entrusted to it. Others therefore can be invited into its recesses, which shrink or expand in response.

The woman, palms still pressed together, shuffles backward, keeping her head bowed. It doesn't even seem to matter to her that the rest of the god's body is elsewhere.

This inner shrine is the smallest room in Elephanta Cave —only about fifteen by fifteen feet. The walls and ceilings are plain stone, remarkable only for the absence of carvings and columns. Just the lingam on its stone, provocateur of war, love, of the irrepressible urge to thrive, to please, to go on, which must rely on the opposing compulsions to destroy, to obliterate, to vie for power. It looks both warm—of blood and body heat—and cool—of stone and cave. If I touch it, I'm afraid it might begin to shudder and swell. I don't do it. I don't even climb onto the platform. The woman lights a small wad of something and places it carefully on the platform, while I stay in the back and watch how the lingam sits, balanced, utterly still, feeling how physical space can seem to close down in a cave, the ceiling bear down, the walls close in while something else seems to get larger, growing, something inside, an interior that seems to have more room at last, that breathes, expands, as if a contraction of the dark exterior opens up an interior until it seems there's more in here than can possibly be held under these stone roofs. I want to crane my head, to look for hinges, pleats, accordion walls, collapsible ceilings, anything to suggest the cave can expand, make room for the spirit as it swells, for the imagination where deities seem to come alive, the inscrutable can stretch, make its own inscrutability more apparent.

In the middle of it all, the poised phallus and the surprising attention I grant it make me wonder if I'm wanting some consolation for what's disappearing or gone: My father is dead, my friend is dying, no man's come into the solitude I too often extol. Across the bay, the beggars put out their hands. They ask. I don't. I'd rather do without than risk the disappointment.

At times my own two intertwined myths—silence and desire—diverge and pull with equal force, the yank in one direction countered by equal and opposite yank in the other, and result in momentary equipoise or paralysis, the roller coaster car paused at the top of the hill, farmlands and forested hills stretched and rolling over what might be below: a whole labyrinth of caves, branching, descending, constricting, cathedral, and always out of sight. It's as if I'm trying to see another dimension, what physically winds beneath the pastures and shopping malls. It's as if I hope there is in each of us some private space I both do and don't want access to, some hidden room from which a force whirls out and spins in and sits entirely still.

Only this is no panorama before me here, no wide perspective from the mountaintop. I'm in a small underground room, a cave whose physical space seems to decrease as some interior expands. How to explain this? To visit Elephanta Cave is to move first across large waters, to climb a mountain, to enter the cave. You go from broad expanse and watery vistas to heights, to an opening, to the outer rock walls alive with the old gods' shudder and dance, to a smaller opening, to lowered ceilings and narrower passages, down to the unadorned center of the shrine, and while the space is contracting around you, leading you into the smaller and smaller, something else is expanding: history and myth, what Chitra would call the great energy of the Hindu gods, what I'd call a spiritual insight that widens the present.

I don't know if this is compensation—the need for expanding room somewhere, anywhere, even inside, as the outside constricts—or simple consequence—what happens when there's no far horizon, no other place to look, no distance to get lost in. You lower your gaze, notice what's around you, maybe even inside you.

I stand watching the lingam, which doesn't move, and the silent devotee, who does, and I think of Frost's short poem: "We dance round in a ring and suppose. / But the Secret sits in the middle and knows."

I wonder if it does. Maybe the secret is that it's impossible to know what's sitting in the middle. Maybe my dad only did what any of us would: ensured his own survival. It's quiet in here. Though I can see the devotee's lips moving slightly, I hear no voice; if she's chanting something, she's chanting silently. I try to imagine what spoken words would seem apt here in such a large, still presence. *Please? Thank you? Glory be? Hallelujah?* Even if I thought there was someone to listen, my words would seem stupid, pointless. Is the woman saying something? What does she hear? Maybe nothing. Her lips move. No words come out. I watch her, expressionless, as she murmurs and bows. I can't tell what she's thinking. I want Chitra to explain her to me, what she's doing, what each gesture means. She tells another Shiva story. The sweat on my back and arms from the long climb up the hill has long since evaporated, left me cool, almost chilled inside the cave. I have no flowers to lay on the lingam, nothing to burn, no coins to offer, nothing to say. The woman has made a final bow to the lingam and left the inner shrine. She's walking toward us and I ask Chitra if we can ask her to talk with me, that I want to understand what she was doing. She shakes her head no.

Shiva fell in love with Parvati because his masquerade allowed her to say how she felt. When they argue, Parvati transforms herself into a mountain maid and orchestrates their reconciliation. Surprises, disguises, no explanations. Just to the left of the inner sanctum's exit, Shiva as the demonic dancer keeps Ravana trapped beneath a mountain. The meaning's never explicated. Nearby sits Ganesha, Shiva's son, whose head the god whacked off and replaced, apologetically, with the big-eared, long-trunked one of an elephant.

The cave isn't full of Shiva's wisdom; it's full of stories, the gods in high drama with the details omitted. There's almost no language here but the language of the body incomplete, the bowing and holding, the marrying and gambling, the missing legs and mouths, the shoulders chipped away. And the woman, too; hers is not the liturgy but the drama of worship, of gestures and offerings. Inside this cave, a woman places a garland of flowers on the phallus of a god. She reaches and bows and bestows and perhaps she doesn't know exactly why. And perhaps this wordless trust she has in what Shiva never says is the incomplete intimacy that keeps her worship alive.

I'm not arguing against language, the sheer force and beauty of words. I'm reminding myself, or maybe just hoping, that some things don't get clearer when they're explained, and might be in fact not just better left unsaid, but more useful left unsaid. The body crumbles, the tongue falls off, the dance goes on. Holding a secret, Jung says, propels a person along his or her own path, intensifies and illuminates the interior life. I think of monks in the frigid cold, hiding a warming stone beneath their robes.

A few nights before he died, my father emerged from his semicomatose state and somehow gestured to his wife that he wanted to make love. No longer able to feed himself, to walk, to talk, he'd been lost for several days in some dark letting-go, but still had this urge, this returning, this rising up in the face of all that was falling away. She told me this story later, marveling at his few moments of final wanting. Was his a typical last request: to reach out in the end not with secrets in hand, but desire? His ashes are on my mantel. Sometimes I touch them, press my fingers into the soft debris of his body. Though at times I want to know what he'd kept hidden, more often it's his choosing not to reveal that I love, the way he carried on the great warmth of his friendships and family while holding some history of himself apart, separate. How it was Eros, not the need to lay bare, that enlivened him even as he died, how maybe his erotic life was made richer, in fact, because of what he did not yield.

The lingam remains still and silent. Passing me on her way out of the cave, the devotee retucks a loose fold in her sari. I can't help myself; I smile at her. She looks at me but does not speak or smile. Out in the hot Indian sun, she slips on her shoes and starts down the long stairway to where the boat must be waiting.

8

DESERT CAVE

I think we are always searching for something
hidden or merely potential or hypothetical,
following its traces whenever they appear on
the surface.
                              — ITALO CALVINO

HALFWAY UP a remote canyon, Kelly spots the mountain lion
track in the dirt of the dry creek bed. "There," she says,
pointing and turning in her saddle to tell Lysa and me, who
are trailing behind her. I look down as my mule and I pass it,
a small, barely noticeable indentation in the soil. Rastus,
picking his way carefully among the rocks, seems oblivious.
Or maybe mules have no fear of mountain lions. Kelly, a professional lion hunter in this high desert country of southeast
Arizona, has taken a day off from her usual obligations to
lead my friend Lysa and me across miles of pastureland and
up a rugged trail to a cave tucked high in the bluffs above the
canyon. I'm interested in the ancient pictographs reported in
the cave. I hadn't bargained for encounters with lions.

"Ghost cats," Native Americans used to call them—

stealthy, shy, superb hunters imbued with spiritual powers and the ability to slip away without a sound. They're often seven to eight feet long, including their tails, and can weigh up to 170 pounds. Pure carnivore. The canyon is dead-quiet except for our occasional talk, the mules' hooves clattering on the stones, the squeak of leather saddles, the rustle of manzanita in the infrequent breeze. Above us and for miles around, nothing appears to move. It seems a land devoid of water, wild animal, anything other than barrenness. But the print indicates otherwise, and I wonder if up in the rocks above us a lion, obscured by shrubbery, follows us with its small eyes.

The history of this land lies above me, not below. There's no need to dig down; the evidence of those millennia-ago geologic events is stacked above in layers of red rock and limestone, in the ancient signs of volcano, the rhyolitic cliffs, the strata of dolostone and black shale. The landscape bears everywhere the signs of erosion and extinction, the inexorable wearing away by water and wind. It's been thousands of years since anything here resembled the fullness of green, the soft earth I'm used to in Appalachia. If anything hides at all here, as the lion might, it's learned to hide itself in spareness, to secret itself behind a pile of bones, blend in with dry brush, erect a camouflage of ghost-colored dust.

Everything seems big here, the landscape, the history, the ranches, the silence, the dryness that makes my lips feel like pencil shavings. I'd driven in last night from Tucson. It was late, an almost-full moon the only light. I had clear directions to Lysa's ranch scribbled on a piece of paper but they didn't include distances. After I'd found the turnoff from Highway 80, I'd started looking for the left-hand turn after two stop signs and three cattleguards, and forty-five minutes later, the road having turned to dirt and not a human or animal in sight, I'd about given up and gone back thirty miles to Tombstone, to Wyatt Earp land and the OK Corral. There were motels back there, streetlights, surely a glass of chilled wine. The desert stretched all around me, its stillness broken only by the dust cloud kicked up by my car. Dark, scorched, fenced and unforgiving. I didn't know what to be wary of. Signs warned travelers of flash floods, but there seemed to be no moisture for miles. There were mountain lions, I was told later, and illegal immigrants moving north in the dark. But I knew none of that at the time. Mostly I was aware of bleakness, the vastness of desert, how unbroken, relentless, and desolate it seemed. This is how it might be, I thought, rolling down the car window, when the comforts of our everyday lives begin to recede, when we're too alone for too long or beginning to die. I could have stopped the car, gotten out, screamed, and nothing would have responded. A tumbleweed might have skittered by. The mountains in the distance would have kept their backs turned, the fence would have gone on and on all the way to the horizon. The occasional cactus would have held its silent vigil.

Out there, my body felt puny, the landscape much too large. I wanted to stretch my arms, touch something. Might such expanse ever be too much? Might people here *need* a cave, the close walls, some sense of enclosure? Living here, maybe you'd want to mark a cave wall simply because you could, because it was close enough, something to touch, a barrier in the vastness of infinity. You could lean against it, claim it, leave a sign in this brutal indifference.

I rolled up the windows, turned the radio on, and kept driving. And suddenly there it was, the turn to the left in the middle of nowhere. The road headed north and then twisted down a series of switchbacks through a steep canyon and out into a valley. I had no idea where I was, how far away the ranch was, what I'd do if I ran out of gas or got a flat tire or took the time to consider what those signs spaced out along the road really meant: "Watch out for animals."

Kelly and her father are a well-known hunting guide team. He'd have been with us this morning too, but a lion had killed a sheep nearby in the night and his contract with the government obligated him to go after it. The trail was fresh; he hadn't been this close to catching this animal that had been killing livestock, and there was no way not to go after it. So they'd split up—he to go after the lion, Kelly to take us up to the cave.

The climb up the canyon is hard. Scrub oaks and cactus clog the trail. Rastus weaves in and out of them, but I haven't learned how to make him avoid the overhanging branches and can only duck when he heads under a low one. I begin to trust him, though, his sure-footedness, the way he seems to consider the careful placement of each hoof. Above us the bluffs rise impossibly high and straight up, slabs of reddish-brown rock with deep vertical folds. Above them, the high blue desert sky, which darkens only for a brief shower and a bit of hail and then brightens again as we keep picking our way up the gorge. Lysa points to a dark stripe high in the bluffs, a vertical streak, caused, I assume, by leaching. It looks like a stain. Lysa thinks of it as a marker, because it's positioned directly above the cave. In fact, we'd seen it miles ago, as we crossed the pastureland. It looked impossibly far off then, several days of hard riding, but no, Kelly had said then, another hour or so and we'd be there. It looms above us now, like an arrow, pointing the way, and we finally leave the canyon floor to scramble up the steep sides. The mules are nimble and steady; all I have to do is hang on as Rastus bounds and lunges and scrambles up the steep talus slope until none of them can go any farther and we stop, dismount, and tie them to shrubs.

My legs feel wobbly, but I don't dare sit down. We're high above the canyon floor, high above the mesa and ravines, the vast palette of gray-beige and rust. There's still the desolation here, the emptiness I'd felt driving in last night, only now I'm closer to it. My feet are on it, rocks under my arches, dust in my nose. Everything seems scrabbly, friable, parched, just the opposite of the land in western Maryland where even in winter the hills are soft and rounded and fuzzed with hemlocks. You can get lost, back home, in all that green. You can pretend there's no end to it, that every next rise will reveal more green, more damp, more shelter. Here it feels as if all wetness has been sucked out of the land. How does anyone dream here without fireflies and the leafy overhang of a bower?

The cave is still above us, another fifteen-minute climb. My boots send small pebbles cascading down the slope as I grab whatever I can—shrubs, a large rock, anything—to keep from sliding down too. "The snakes have been bad this year," Kelly warns us over her shoulder. "Watch where you put your feet." I'm two seconds behind her and I put mine exactly where she puts hers.

Miles from anywhere and almost six thousand feet up in the bluffs, this cave doesn't invite visitors. Who, I wonder, would have made this trek? Who would've hiked or ridden and climbed through such harsh country to scramble around a last few boulders and into a dark alcove that couldn't have sheltered more than a dozen people for a couple of days? And why? I know about this cave only because it's on Lysa's ranch. She's been here, shown me pictures, encouraged me to visit. My boot sends another stone skittering down the slope as I scramble around another oak, and suddenly there's a bighorn sheep in front of me and a pack of dogs and over there a deer, and under it a something with a tail that winds up and over its back. The dark bodies seem to move all over the cave wall. Some combination of sunlight and shadow and the odd angles of all the creatures, the slanting this way and that of the various grounds you have to imagine them standing on, running on, leaping on, make it seem as if they're all alive.

You can see them even before you're in the cave, whose entrance evokes none of the fear I've felt before. This mouth is wide; daylight spills inside and the cave is shallow, the first wall no more than six feet from the entrance. There's a rock at the opening I try leaning against. My legs are still trembly, my backside sore. I can't get comfortable and finally slide down to sit on the ground. In front of me, the dogs' long ears stand up; some are cocked, others curled. Their mouths are open, their expression a cross between ferocious and comic. The deer and sheep turn their heads or they look up; they're poised to run or their feet are firmly planted.

Some of them look like the drawings a child does in first or second grade, thick and clumsy fingers having titled them in green crayon: "This is my dog" or "My pet cat." Only the artists here wouldn't have been children, the tool not crayon, the drawings not easily taped to refrigerator doors. They're not stick figures. They're solid, filled in with charcoal pigment.

When I finally get up and walk inside, I'm immediately stopped by the stink of bat shit. It lies in thick drifts, spilling from the back corners out across the cave floor like a glacier of guano creeping toward the edge of the cliff. How old is this stuff? How long does it take to develop that telltale odor of ammonia? Whatever colony deposited it isn't here today, would, I assume, have left weeks ago for winter grounds elsewhere. I go out to the entrance for a moment to gulp fresh air. The cave itself is small, with two rooms, one about fifteen by twenty feet, the other about six by nine. There's no squirming here, no rappelling down abysses, no turning sideways to fit anywhere. It looks as if someone with a giant ice cream scoop had dipped twice into the cliffs. The floor is fairly level, sloping up just a bit as you walk farther into the recess. It's a dry cave, though there's evidence that water had once leaked through, left an array of what seemed to be tiny stalactites in the ceiling, a spray of dusty sequins with the luster long gone.

On the wall closest to me is a picture of an animal with antlers and bifurcated feet, and so probably a deer. Next to it, what look like sheep, their horns curving backward, and then something humanlike, though it looks two-headed to me, with arms that fade from solid black to dotted. Studies of petroglyphs—engravings—and pictographs—paintings—all over the West have suggested their importance to various indigenous cultures. But the figures here are unusual. According to the one study done on them, they don't fit the pattern of other rock art in the area. The absence of key elements —horses and expanded midbodies and abstract markings, for example—and the presence of others—eyes and mouths —make it difficult to classify them as Hohokam or Mogollon or Mimbres, the most likely nearby rock art styles.

Many petroglyphs are scratched into the desert varnish that coats ancient rocks. The varnish—thought to be a combination of remnants of dead bacteria mixed with iron-manganese salts leached from the rock—is dark, so that when the artist cuts thin lines in it, he exposes the lighter rock beneath. On those walls, what appears as outlines of deer, bison, and sheep some thousands of years later, then, is the older rock visible as etchings. The dust and dead bacteria, of course, begin to accumulate almost immediately, graying the newly exposed stone, obscuring the outline. It could be that thousands of petroglyphs lie undetected beneath later layers of the varnish. They could be hidden here in this cave, too, alongside these very visible drawings.

The midafternoon sun shines directly against the outermost walls. The figures look as vivid and bold as if they'd been painted there last year. Though some markings are obviously recent, most of them are prehistoric. Radiocarbon dating puts them somewhere between 500 B.C. and 500 A.D. Some two thousand years ago, before Cortez, before Coronado, a group of people made their way up this canyon, which would have been much greener then, forested, without these scrubby oaks and cacti. They clambered up the canyon and took a piece of charcoal and drew images on the wall.

I know the paintings weren't done to help a child — or anyone — learn how imagination and a good eye can produce something pleasing. In fact, most speculation about the origins of pictographs rules out the "art for art's sake" theory. The remoteness of the cave suggests that it would've been visited by only a fraction of the culture that created it. Large-tribe ceremonies would probably never have taken place here. So why? An appeal to the hunting gods to provide game? The result of a shaman's trance to reduce risk to hunters? Self-eulogy? Doodling?

Some of the drawings are isolated, disconnected, images with no context. Others have more of a sense of story. The characters' positions relative to each other suggest chase or herding or triumph. In one, a human's eyes are not painted but sunken; the artist drew the face around a pair of natural pits in the wall. The figure looks haunted, maybe hunted. Or are we looking as if from inside his skull, and he's the one, face to the wall, peering even further into the stone?

Kelly uses the toe of her boot to dig a bit in the guano. She's looking for dried wads of spoonlily cactus that she's found in other caves. "The Indians chewed it like tobacco," she explains. "Sometimes you can find it with tooth marks still visible." A few of the figures are pale gray, almost ghostly on the rock. And here's one—I get up and look at it closely—that appears comically burdened with a tail three times the length of its body. "Mountain lion," Kelly says, looking around. "They're everywhere in here." I follow her gaze. On the wall across the larger room, another one, this too with a long tail. And back toward the smaller room, a couple more, their tails again curved back over the bodies. Some of them are more than a foot long. I count at least ten.

I know that mountain lions once ranged all over the West and that in most places their populations have diminished over the last decades. I've read that in Mohave mythology, the mountain lion is the Creator's helper. I know they're fairly secretive animals, loners, nocturnal like most cats, and sometimes a menace to ranchers, that they like to ambush from behind, sink their teeth into the base of the skull. I think of the paw print in the canyon below us, and of Kelly's father out hunting the one that had killed a sheep last night, her walkie-talkie crackling a while ago with the message they'd tracked it up some gulch.

I don't yet have a private mythology for the mountain lion. Whatever story might evolve will be new, something I'm likely to create today. Raised on the East Coast where they've been absent for a hundred years, I have no long associations, no needs, no stories, no fear or kinship. Armed with charcoal pigment and preliterate mind, I wouldn't draw a mountain lion. Or the coatimundi Kelly tells me one figure is, a raccoonlike creature I'd never heard of. I'd draw what I lived with—white-tailed deer, black bear—or what was most on my mind—dinner, children, storm clouds.

Out the mouth of the cave, I can see the panorama of hill and butte and canyon that stretches on for miles and miles. I can see the canyon I traveled up this morning, and beyond it the pastureland I crossed hours ago, and beyond that the mountains I snaked down last night to reach the ranch, now hidden behind another rise of bluffs. Miles and miles of high desert. I don't know which pulls more: the inward view of the cave with its history, its mysterious drawings, its blackened ceiling, its lore of shamans and outlaws and stink of bat shit. Or the outward view with its long vista and desolate beauty.

Some researchers speculate that the pictographs here are a marker to a way of life that, for those who felt the need to draw them, was about to disappear. They must have been responding to the shift from a hunter-gatherer culture to an agricultural one. I want to believe this theory, but know of no other culture with such historical perspective. It implies both a detachment and a vision that seem, even in this landscape, unlikely. How could they have known? How, in the up-close midst of our daily lives, can any of us ever tell what will stay, what will go? Any of us, that is, except our artists, who may have no idea what motivates them, other, perhaps, than the impulse to draw something, say something. I study the drawing of father and son and wonder about them, who they were, what they did.

Lysa, a visual artist, shoots a whole roll of film. She's just finished a series of paintings of horses lying down, maybe dead or exhausted, their hipbones positioned awkwardly, legs splayed, heads down on the desert floor. She's been interested in how grace and power collapse. I don't know what she sees here; I don't know whether she does either, or whether she's just "following traces," as Italo Calvino says, "whenever they appear on the surface."

Some of what's traced on the surface here are hunting stories. A dog rounding up a bunch of sheep. A deer with an arrow through its belly. The father and son next to each other appear to be a hunting team. I think of Kelly and her dad. She's six feet tall with warm brown eyes and blond hair in a single braid to her waist. She wears a cowboy hat and leather chaps, a smile that could dazzle-stop a rattler, and a pistol on her hip.

I hadn't noticed it earlier or hadn't known what it was—a honey-colored pouch fastened to her belt. She lets me hold it. It feels heavy in my hand, a .357 Ruger, a sleek contraption of steel and chambers and a barrel I raise and point out over the canyon below. I try to imagine a mountain lion charging me. Or a mountain lion slinking off into the brush with a sheep carcass in its mouth. Or just slinking off, trying to remain unseen. Kelly says they often track them for days, following prints, the dogs with their noses to the ground. They're secretive and sly. Beautiful, a blur of tawny power. And hungry, intent on staying alive. I wonder whether I could aim and shoot.

One of the pictographs in the larger room of the cave shows a man with a bow and arrow in his left hand and an animal in his right. It's impossible to read the expression on his face, mouth and eyes wide open: triumph? gratitude? trepidation? Did he ask the gods to bless his hunt? Give thanks when the arrow thunked into the animal's chest? What does Kelly do?

A mountain lion devours livestock, slips away in the underbrush. Even when track and carcass indicate its nearby presence, it remains almost invisible. This is its home. I can almost sense one watching us. The ghost cat frequents these hills; its image haunts this cave. I almost wish I'd known, driving through all that desolate beauty last night, that there could be lions around. It would have been, in some strange way, a comfort, something warm in an empty place. Hunting always means awareness of the other. Someone's behind you or ahead of you. Your every move takes the other's presence into account. You elude or quicken; you climb or step side-ways. You and something else are alive out there. There's a trail and that means choices, something to plan from. Should you track or veer off? Does knowing where they are encourage or console? Or frighten? Better to be in a trackless desert or one imprinted by something, even if it's elusive or deadly?

I'm beginning to like knowing the lion might be somewhere in this canyon. It's beginning to matter to me.

When the light turns golden, slant, we gather our things and start down. Rastus appears to be sleeping on his feet when we approach. His long lashes sweep up over huge brown eyes as he opens them and stands still while I swing my leg up and over, as if I'd been doing this for years. On the way back down the canyon, I realize I've already learned better how to guide him, pulling him left or right, now comfortable enough even to lift one hand off the horn and hold branches aside as we clomp through overhanging brush.

Halfway down, Kelly spots another lion track and then another. "Female," she says. What she sees clearly, I can barely make out. She points out the spread toe prints. Then the clouds shift and the late afternoon sun illuminates the rim of one print and deepens its shadows. It's suddenly as visible as the cave paintings. "How long ago?" I ask, staring, not sure what answer to hope for. "An hour? Two?" "Oh no," Kelly laughs, "that lion's long gone. Hasn't been in this canyon for at least a day, maybe two."

I look more closely. I can almost see the big paw lowered, the gritty dirt pressed or shifting sideways, the small ridge formed as her weight bore down, the light sand splayed as her flanks rippled forward and she lifted her foot. All afternoon, I'd been feeling watched by what had disappeared days ago.

DERICHMENT

It is this backwards motion toward the source,
against the stream, that most we see ourselves in.
                                        — ROBERT FROST

IN THE DEEPEST known part of a cave in southern Virginia, I turn off my headlamp and walk slowly forward, straining my eyes, looking for anything, any shadow, any small fluctuation in the amount of darkness, the shape of black against blacker. My right foot bangs against a small rock; my right arm swings out, finds the wet wall, and steadies me. I stand still for a moment, trying to see something, anything. Nothing. Because I'd told her I wanted to see how it was in the dark by myself, Jenny, the guide I'd hired, has left me here, swung the strap of her bag over her shoulder and disappeared down some passageway. I'd heard her feet on the cave floor, not the clicking of heels on tile, but the grind and shuffle of boot on gravelly, uneven rock. She'd moved away slowly, cautiously, deliberately, as one must in a cave, the beam of her light bobbing in front of her feet, each step a little more muffled and distant until I couldn't hear her at all and only the invisible drip-drip from the ceiling broke the absolute silence. It's completely, utterly dark in here.

Maybe for every younger twin, the sound of departure means a little solitary room at last. Perhaps for me, those thirteen minutes finally alone in the womb with the chance to uncross my arms and stretch out spindly legs have left me forever interested in the moments just after something large has gone. Surely I must have felt the stillness—my sister has always been more active, more physically alert and responsive, than I—and maybe some lessening of water-muffled noise, her nearby sloshing in the sac gone, leaving me better able to hear my mother's heartbeat or my own. Did I roll around? Turn upside down? Have a few minutes of dizziness? Does a sudden leaving both sensitize and disorient?

Driving to the airport after my father died, I felt my internal compass go haywire. I got lost, headed west when I should have gone east, missed exits off the interstate, couldn't use the sun to figure out direction. It was as if I had always had him as a north pole, a force to set my compass by, a steady North Star for navigation. Deprived of his voice, his presence, his birthday cards and good wishes, the stories of his adventures, I could not, for weeks, get my bearings.

We use landscape and the people in our lives to orient ourselves. We know which window the morning sun comes through; we know on the East Coast that storms usually arrive from the West; Muslims know where Mecca is, Native Americans where the sun rises; we know what the Saturday paper on the doorstep means, what to do about a certain sullenness in the one we love.

Take all that away. Remove the sun, the east-running rivers, the routines and daily reminders. Put yourself in a chamber of absence, where there's nothing that says aim west, offer an apology, schedule an oil change, remember to bring in more firewood. It's dark and empty, unpopulated, its features invisible. Maybe what I want in this cave is some slow motion, embodied drama of disorientation and adieu, the chance to study in isolated detail how it feels when almost everything's gone: when your twin's born first, when people leave, when the footsteps stop, when the rain ends.

There's a lot that's absent here: changing weather, sun, rain, visible plant life, clouds, sky, the possibility of horizon. It's the same all over the world—in France, China, New Zealand—you go inside a cave and you know that something major is missing. The indigenous creatures, of course, have had thousands of years to adjust, generation by generation, to what remains after the slow washing out, to the water trickling through tiny cracks, widening, carving, dissolving the limestone, carting it away in subterranean streams. For me, however, used to daylight and green, the absence today is sudden, and I turn my light back on to walk farther down the dank passage. The guide had told me that ahead, off to the side and running parallel to the main passage, is a narrow crevice, small enough to twist your ankle, too small in most places to fall bodily into. I keep my headlamp aimed in front of my feet and swing my flashlight back and forth across the floor. It bounces off boulders, rockchunks, the muddy floor, searching out a jagged streak, a gash of darker at the edge of dark. "Listen for it," she'd told me. What did she mean by that? I couldn't imagine the sound a crevice might make. Does it creak, like a stone yawn? The ceiling drips, my feet shuffle; everything else is silent.

I'm trying to understand how the mind works when it's subjected to subtraction and absence. Do we become less flexible or more grounded? Bored by the tedium of deletion or less moody? delusional or less superficial? The cave itself is an argument against the claim that growth requires variety and accumulation. It doesn't grow by a flurry of new processes or added weight, substance, or multiplying cells. No huge flood, no volcanic eruption, no earthquake. You can count on a limestone cave's existence being the result of millions of years of the exact same process. The cave is about erasure and exodus, the humdrum routine of taking away. The rain drips through bedrock, dissolves a bit of stone, dissolves a little more.

My children's kindergarten was in a new elementary school. The rooms were all bright, the furniture was bright; bright plastic modular units were frequently moved around on sound-absorbent carpeting to change the shape of the classroom space. There were always new things to touch, to manipulate. My daughter learned about plants by growing moss in a terrarium, about air currents by flying kites. My son studied other cultures by crawling inside life-sized teepees and making masks. It was a rich environment, the school all clean and shiny and colorful and stimulating.

They each left that school after kindergarten to attend a four-room schoolhouse way out in the country. Though part of the public school system, it was run by Mennonites who welcomed all kids in grades one through eight, including children, like my own, who weren't attached to any particular faith. The school was old. Its floors were wooden; the desks were old and wooden and scratched. There was a certain spareness to the atmosphere, a few experiments growing on windowsills, but a lot of white walls, brown floor, big windows, wide spills of uninterrupted light.

And books. Lots and lots of books. If you wanted to learn about other cultures, you read about them in books. About science and math and history, books. Reading was the one steady, repeated, reliable method of teaching and learning. A lot of silent reading periods, a lot of being read to aloud. In subject after subject, written language was the medium. It streamed into their heads, carved patterns in their brains, deepened the neural pathways of language acquisition. The children in the school might not have been whizzes at the video arcade or computer games. The school was, in fact, an argument against excessive variety, against the belief that children learn best in an active, animated atmosphere of constantly changing stimuli.

I suspect what the school did was teach them to deepen their attention. They learned how it felt not to have various stimuli competing for attention. They learned to bring the whole mind to the task at hand. How to concentrate their mental powers on the one task that required it. I see the lack of this ability in many of my students today. They want to bring all kinds of rip-rap into their writing, everything that happened to them one night in a bar, in a bed, at the family reunion. Fine, for an early draft, I tell them. But before they bring it to class I want them to pay close attention to what's really going on in the writing. What's the underlying thread? What *doesn't* belong? What's between the noisier lines? What can we not quite hear? Used to handling so many stimuli at once, they struggle to slow the juggling, even to know the value and reward of zeroing in on one subtle idea. I want to bring them into a cave, set them up in a small cranny for a few weeks, get them used to listening to less noise, have them learn to focus their attention.

If they stayed long enough, generation after generation, they'd grow accustomed to the dark. They wouldn't, like nocturnal animals, develop keener eyesight for nighttime hunting. They'd lose it. Their eyes would shrink, atrophy.

Their optic nerve would lie in their heads, useless, like an appendix. And then their pigment would go. Their skin, all that honey-colored, coffee, pearly flesh they so love to show off in tank tops and shorts, would fade, grow pallid, blanched. Their shells would thin, their defenses grow delicate. I imagine them, Chad and Danielle and the others, curled with their notebooks in the nooks my headlamp is darting in and out of. I imagine visiting them there, consulting, advising, and departing. They'd feel all this as loss, of course, their world diminished. I wonder what kind of poems they'd offer in exchange.

A few minutes later I hear something, some movement in the stillness. Something low, muffled, but definitely there and I stumble a little faster, following the noise, until the beam of my flashlight arcs over an edge, a long, scraggy brink. The crevice isn't wide, maybe three feet at the top, but deep. My light finds the bottom and the source of the noise: sixty or seventy feet below, a small stream flows. It's narrow, maybe a foot wide, a few inches deep, though it's hard to tell, flowing down there in the skinny dark.

Hard to tell, too, what's living down there and therefore easy to imagine the need to mythologize. In the seventeenth century, for example, the people of Slovenia scooped up white, lizardlike creatures from the waters that flowed from nearby caves and believed they were holding the larvae of dragons in their hands. It took years for the stories of cave monsters to settle into the fact of eyeless, albino salamanders and, in this country, it wasn't until the mid-1850s that speleobiologists—cave biologists—began to study the adaptations of troglobites—creatures that spend their whole lives in the darkness of a cave. Troglobites have no choice about this; they cannot survive in the sunlit world. They cannot even manage the twilight zone. They need total, constant dark.

And they've needed it for generations, been resolute in their avoidance of light, even as their eyes deteriorated, their shells thinned, their bodies gave up what didn't matter anymore in the dark.

The process of loss differs from one species to another. The cavefish *Typhlichthys*, for example, still has remnants of an eye lens, but no muscle to move it. The *Amblyopisi* has remnants of eye muscle, but no lens and, hence, nothing for the muscle to move. The Ozark blind salamander is actually born with small eyes, but its eyelids soon shut and fuse together. What's trapped beneath may twitch and bulge for a while but will soon give up, begin to shrink. Most likely, generations from now, those short-lived larval eyes will have deteriorated to the point that the embryo no longer develops them. Some troglobite brains have changed shape, and cave beetles don't even have optic nerves anymore.

Cave-dwelling creatures lose more than eyesight. They lose their thick shells and they lose their pigment. Aboveground creatures produce shells and pigment as protective strategy. Armor protects, not only against other creatures, but also against cold and rain, the normal fluctuations of weather. Darker coloring blends in with rocks, mud, tree bark, and underbrush and makes prey less visible to predator. To produce chitin and pigment requires energy, a necessary expenditure in the aboveground, clawed, and bitten world, and so the animal world responds in its feathered, scaly, furred, stippled, spotted, hued, and shadowed way.

Heavy protection from unstable weather, however, is irrelevant inside the cave. And camouflage is useless in an environment where nobody can see anybody anyway, so most troglobites don't waste their energy. Their shells are thin and most creatures are born pale, even translucent, and spend their whole lives as albinos on dark stone walls, in black underground rivers. The cave crayfish is pearly; the cavefish looks like a cigar-shaped peeled onion with fins. Troglobitic salamanders resemble pale and starving four-legged slugs, while millipedes are as white as the early shoots of nasturtiums unburied in spring gardens.

I confess they're creepy. It's more than their ghostliness. More than the remembered fear of an albino child in our neighborhood when we were young, her pale lashes and otherworldiness, the way she looked too delicate to ride on a school bus but did anyway. It's knowing that the troglobites' delicacy helps them survive in an environment that would kill a human, that they can, in fact, use their faint ways to out-compete a sighted, thick-skinned competitor for food. I'm used to the merits of heartiness, robustness. If I were looking for a mate, evolutionary biologists tell me, I'd be looking for good size and color, both indicators of health and the ability to protect our offspring. If I had children in mind, I'm less likely to choose a blind male with thin skin, someone inclined to spend his days indoors with the shades drawn. And yet, developing those same qualities—that is, losing the normal indicators of vigor—is what enables the cave-dwellers to survive. They are, in their blind, belowground world, the contradiction to those accustomed to succeeding in the unstable, fiercely competitive world aboveground.

Cave-dwellers compensate for their lack of vision by enhancing their feeling receptors. They grow longer, touch-sensitive antennae. They also sprout shorter, chemo-sensitive antennae. On their heads, cavefish develop four times the number of sense organs—called neuromasts—as their aboveground counterparts do. And those four-times-as-many organs are all more than twice as sensitive, enabling a blind cavefish to sense a water flea at three times the distance its sighted counterpart can. Troglobites have larger odor sensors, better balance mechanisms, larger vibration receptors in their brains.

In a world without sun, sky, rain, eyeballs, thick skins, and pigment, how do they survive? By knowing what they feel, by a heightened sense of touch. Staying alive in a cave means listening to your skin. Eyesight doesn't help, nor does the brilliance of your plumage, the swell of your chest, or whether you can make your throat blush and balloon with mating-croaks. Camouflage means nothing. Nobody who lives here can see a thing. If you stay long enough, you drop it all, the excesses, the decorations, the visible markings we animals use to advertise our potential as mates or to evade our enemies. You grow pale, almost translucent. Loss, in other words, can enhance your sensitivity, make your insides more apparent.

In the troglobitic world, it takes thousands of years. After the initial retreat to a cave, a species' devolution is slow, gradual, a gene here, a gene there. It took millions of generations for crayfish to lose their eyes and lengthen their antennae. Who knows how many perished in the first stages of the experiment, unable to see in the dark, unequipped yet with compensatory feelers, starving while some eight-legged meal crept nearby? Or, early on, how many suffered from the too-sudden effects of sensory deprivation, the absence of light, rain, sky. If you take a young rat, a mostly nocturnal creature, and whack off its whiskers, it's unable as an adult to master certain learning tasks. It can't compensate for the lack of information its whiskers would normally transmit. If you catch an adult mole, accustomed to life in the dirt, and snip off its whiskers, it becomes not only learning-impaired, but neurotic. If you take a human and put him in a sensory deprivation chamber, he's prone to hallucinations and odd behaviors. I once knew a man who volunteered for such an experiment. The researchers put him on a table in a small room, encased his arms and legs in long cardboard tubes, blindfolded him, put earphones on him that issued a steady stream of white noise, turned off the lights, and left him alone for hours. He lay quietly at first, wishing he hadn't been out drinking the night before. And then as the deprivation lengthened, he began to resist it. At first he tried lifting his long cardboard arms and banging them together. Then his legs. Then arm to leg, leg to arm until nothing seemed enough, and small dots of light started to appear. Other subjects reported squiggles, a line of dogs, a procession of open mouths. The speculation is that the brain in such a sensory void eventually begins to compensate, to create images where there are none.

This need to fill a sudden void is what brainwashers count on. After months of solitary confinement with nothing but propaganda to fill in the blanks, the mind gets confused, has trouble sorting out what's real, what's not. Interrogators in prisoner-of-war camps know this, as do cult leaders, maybe even some proponents of prolonged meditation. Reducing external stimuli can produce altered states of consciousness, including visual and auditory illusions, and sometimes feelings of expansiveness, great waves of love and tranquility. Who knows what happened in the small minds of those first cave-dwelling creatures, what kind of hallucinatory compensation they might have experienced?

I think of Emily Dickinson, not blind, but pale and delicate, a white-dressed recluse in her room, a woman who seldom left Amherst, increasingly avoided the excesses of ocean, the populations and panoply of nearby Boston, who gradually intensified her austere seclusion and knew every inch of the heart's interior. Every nuance, every side passage and hidden crevice of the emotional underworld, a world she mined for poems so startlingly clear they read like beacons in a once-shrouded landscape.

One afternoon, Jeanne lay on her bed and told me everything she didn't do anymore. Some of them were things she couldn't, physically, manage: her career as a statistical expert for the National Science Foundation, travel to China, the weeds in the garden, washing the car. But some things she stopped because she simply didn't wish to do them anymore. She no longer answered her phone, e-mails, letters. She didn't watch television or look through her dozens of fat photo albums. We'd shared a great love of reading all our lives, but on most afternoons now, she told me, she simply lay in bed with the book on her lap. "Do you go back over your life?" I asked. "Think about regrets or good moments?" "Sometimes," she answered. "But more often, even on good days, I just lie here and don't think about anything. I just lie here." She smiled. "I'm just here."

I knew she wanted me to understand this, how it feels to know it's time to put things down, to stop. I knew, too, that I couldn't understand that, or I couldn't feel it as she felt it. I did, however, know that I was in the presence of some big thing happening. Being with a woman who has, after a long battle, accepted the fact that her death is imminent made me feel how much I deny mine, made me feel how achingly I want years ahead of me, how naïve and stubborn and defiant I can feel. She was dying and she felt her end, which she didn't resist anymore. She wasn't bitter, was no longer angry. I wanted to talk about junior high school, how Belinda Izzi lit up a cigarette in the school library. Remember that? Or the way Mr. Bell warned us about liking boys too much? I asked her. I wanted our memories, like a transfusion, to keep our lives going, to keep us alive together, as if a stream of remembered images could somehow get inside her body, dissolve the tumors, leave her rinsed and ready for another twenty years.

She smiled at me. Her body was crowded with cancer and fluids and drugs. Her mind was astonishingly clear. If she wanted anything, it was to give away. "Here," she said, handing me a small jeweled box from Thailand, "take this. And this." She was, it seemed, being rinsed after all. While her body broke down, her mind was somehow growing more uncluttered. Sitting with her, I could almost feel that she'd grown more unjumbled, more smooth, fluid; I could almost sense something untangling itself, running unimpeded now, out of her, away from her. It wasn't that flowing thing that felt so rarified; it was what remained, how the leaving had created in her such thinned, almost pure space. I was sure she must know things now that none of us not face-to-face with our deaths can know. *What?* I wanted to ask her. *Tell me.* But I didn't, couldn't. Probably wouldn't have understood even if she could have answered.

A week later I opened the gate at the entrance of a crevice-cave in New England and stepped into a stream that rushed toward me, eddied around my boots, flowed on behind me, year after year, out of the cave, out of the mountain, that tumbled away, down over its slopes. Even in wool socks, my feet got cold. I walked into the cave against the stream's current, back and back in the dark between high, narrow walls the water had cut over thousands of years. I was walking toward something, I didn't know what. Toward the source of water? There was no source. There was only the knee-deep water that ran in a current and had, some time ago, seeped through from the ground above and, before that, fallen as rain and before that evaporated from the oceans and before that run in riverbeds, in streams, inside caves, maybe had even been in that one before. I walked and walked; the cave became chasm; it twisted and wound and the walls got narrower; I could stretch out my arms and touch them on both sides. There were few formations and the stream was still cold.

Monotony is the backdrop of most meditations. You sit on your cushion and you sit and sit and sit. Nothing happens. You watch your thoughts; you let them go. Monks all over the East have for thousands of years meditated in caves. In 1976, an English woman climbed into a cave in the Himalayas and for twelve years she mostly sat. She ate rice and lentils, a few vegetables, a bit of bread, a few bites of tsampa. She sat and sat and the cave stayed cold and the stream stayed cold, but the chasm deepened and this, I suppose, is what meditation is about. You learn to watch and let go, watch and let go.

No more bullshit, Jeanne says.

A deriched environment? Maybe. Certainly Jeanne isn't accumulating anymore, materially or physically. She's discarding, letting go, letting things slough off. But she's not turning airy, ethereal, wraithlike. In fact, the more frail her body becomes, the more grounded her mind seems, more able to sort what matters from what doesn't. She grows tired of my need for memories, wants me to just sit and hold her hand. I do this for hours, watching her fade and return. She loves the feel of my fingers on her palm, her thin arms. Her dying doesn't disorient me, or free up a little more room, or offer hope for some new beginning. Part of me feels carried along on her slow, cell-by-cell closing down and flowing out, and part of me has one hand on the stone and clay in a cave that I love, walking farther in, following the stream to its source, hunting albino shrimp, a sightless salamander.

I can hear Jenny's footsteps for a full five minutes before I see her light. She's been exploring some side rooms, but wants to take me now to a specific passage in the cavern. I lift my pack to my shoulders and we walk and walk. The cavern twists and narrows, grows wide, grows low. Sometimes we scramble; sometimes we walk fairly easily. I have no idea where we are. Fifteen minutes later she leads me around a bend and into a side passage, and suddenly my hair, light and curly in the humidity, lifts away from my ears. I look at her in amazement and then turn and face it—what?—directly. Wisps of her hair lift off her neck, too. There's a light wind here, deep below the surface, a wind that smells distinctively *old*, meaning, perhaps, that it's been underground awhile, like the air in catacombs, mausoleums, underground parking garages with poor ventilation. Jenny grins and shines her flashlight at me, watching the wispy tendrils puff around my head. Then it stops. Then I feel it from behind, as if someone has circled behind me and is breathing down my neck, sending tendrils forward over my ears, surrounding my face like a wimple. "This is a breathing cave," she tells me. A breathing cave? We stand still; in a couple of minutes my hair reverses direction again, lifts away from my forehead now.

We are standing in the entrance of the small passageway, maybe four feet wide. The muddy stone walls lean toward us. Changes in barometric pressure or wind turbulence near the cave's main entrance often cause the air to move even deep inside a cave. Sometimes you barely notice it. Sometimes the right configuration of multiple entrances produces a breeze you can feel lightly on your skin. There are even blowing caves where winds whip out the entrance at forty miles an hour. In a breathing cave, however, air moving across the entrance to a smaller passage, such as the one Jenny and I are standing in, acts the way your breath does if you position your lips just so and blow into a Coke bottle.

The movement of air across the bottle's narrow neck produces high-frequency sound waves. You hear the bottle hum. Down here, the high volume of air moving across the entrance to this smaller passage produces low-frequency waves, which means no sound, just the periodic flow reversals, oscillations that resemble breathing and lift my hair one way and then the other.

No wonder so many yogis meditated in caves. You can imagine their deep breathing in here, feel the slow, deep inhalations. I remember my Indian guide Sunithi trying to teach me about breath and its relation to wind. Hindus, she explained, have arranged the five elements in hierarchical order. At the bottom is earth, which we can touch, see, hear, taste, and shape. Next up is water, which we can touch, see, hear, and taste, but not shape. And then fire, which we can neither touch nor shape. And then wind, which we can only feel; and finally space, which we cannot see, feel, touch, taste, or shape, but whose existence we cannot deny. Through fasting, that ancient, Eastern practice of nutritional derichment, she explained, one might realize the power of the body and ascend the hierarchy of elements. It is through that ascension, leaving behind earth, water, and fire and concentrating on wind and space, that one might, she said, approach the divine.

With the breath first on my face, then the back of my neck, I don't know much about the divine, unless it's those moments, alone or with another, when defenses crumble and you feel transparent, your interiors exposed. When to inch ahead is not even a matter of vision, when you go on and on, led only by what you feel, and what you feel if you're lucky is some enormous expansiveness, an upswelling and the swoosh of what can drop away, leaving you exposed, every part of your body both alert and permeable and what you want most, finally, is to give it all away. Here, you say, *take this and this,* and I don't know if this is how Jeanne feels, dying, or whether when my father died he'd handed over the invisible compass I didn't know how to use on my own, left me disoriented, headed in all the wrong ways. *Take this and this* and finally I did, I took it, and west settled back into west and east, east; and now I'm interested again in wind, how even my rudimentary understanding of what causes the breathing doesn't erase my sense that the cave *is* breathing and that though I love the mind at work, its theories and tangents, its draw to paradox, I'm interested now in the opposite, too: the unadorned, distilled, pared down to what I thought was the core, the thing itself without its layers of hiding and flesh. Peel away the layers of an onion and what you get down to is something oblong and pearly, not a core, a seed, or a bone that says the beginning, but the last layer of succulence, a cluster of veined petals, a nest of opalescence.

The cave breathes. My hair lifts one way and then the other. There's no fire in here, no earth we can shape. No sun, no moon, no green, no day. The beings who live here survive because of how they've adapted to what they've lost. Blind, transparent, they rely on highly tuned receptors. They survive by knowing what they feel. "Touch me," the poet Stanley Kunitz pleads, "remind me who I am." "Hold my hand," Jeanne says again.

In the bottom waters of this cave stream, Jenny confirms, blind albino shrimp wiggle their way underground. Their shells have thinned over thousands of years, their antennae grown long. All over their backs, their sides, hundreds of small receptors keep their bodies alert. I think of the photograph at home of a troglobitic cave shrimp. It looks like a transparent ghost with many feelers, an oblong made of plastic wrap. Inside it, clearly visible, an orangy mass that must be its brain, maybe its heart.

10

RESCUE

... the depths in every consciousness from
which we cannot rescue ourselves — to which
none can go with us.
— EMILY DICKINSON

A YOUNG MAN is trapped far back in a cave. He has a headlamp with low batteries, a little water, and a leg that's
wedged in a tight spot. A couple of hours ago, his companion
left to try to get help; he has plenty of time to consider his
dilemma. What does he do? How does he handle this?

Emily, one of the top cave rescue experts in the country,
asks me this question about a neighbor who got caught in a
cave a couple of years ago. We're walking through a light
woods in upstate New York toward a cave where today she's
supervising a mock rescue operation. It's also the cave with
the Gun Barrel in one of the lower chambers that she wants
to show me, a long, almost straight tube through stone.
When you kneel down and look through it, she says, it appears to get smaller and smaller toward its far end. I've been
reading about Baby Jessica, who got stuck in a well, and how

not everyone who gets caught in a squeeze gets out. I consider the predicament of the young man, who is a philosophy student. I consider his physical needs and his psychological needs, and wonder whether his training would help, whether it's possible to be philosophical about waiting immobilized in the dark. What I'm really wondering is what I'd do and what I'd think about if I were similarly trapped.

I've waited alone in a cave several times and have, in fact, recently made that solitude one of my self-imposed tests-in-a-cave. The second time I did it was in a Pennsylvania cave. I knew the others would be back in an hour or so; I wasn't hurt or lost, but I wanted to imagine that I was. The entrance to the cave was two hours up and away from the room where I stayed. A fairly large room, maybe twenty by twenty. The beam of my headlamp revealed several darker holes—passages out of the room—one a small arched opening, another a cockeyed space under a jumble of rock. I swung my flashlight around: over there a low crawlway, up there what looked like an open trap door to an attic. The first thing I was aware of was that I had no idea which passage I had come through just ten minutes ago. I closed my eyes and tried, in my mind, to reverse my body's movements. Had I just scrambled and dropped down from a higher opening? Or had I just been crawling? Or walking stooped? I'd done all of that in the last two hours, my body reminded me, but I had no idea of the sequence, could not put those movements in reverse and go back the way I'd come. Maybe a dancer could do it, knew locomotion as a series of separate movements—arabesque, leap, chassé, knee-bends—that could be stopped, played back, resumed, fine-tuned, perfected, repeated, reversed, torso and legs going backward through the sequence the body remembered, back off the stage, out of the cave, into the sunlight and fresh air, but I couldn't. Neither my body nor my mind had any idea where I'd just come from. I sat down and, by the light of the beam, studied the options. No clues in any of them, no muddy footprints, shreds of clothing caught on tree branches, no broken twigs. Stone is unforgiving, impervious, leaves no trace of who, if anyone, has just passed by.

Emily shakes her head at me when I finish this story. "Big mistake," she says, stepping over a branch on the trail. I step over it too, follow her as she takes a smaller path to the right. We pass two men standing just off the path, a map unfolded between them. Emily greets them, but does not introduce me. We keep walking. "Good thing you weren't really alone in there or lost. You made one of the big ones." I don't want to seem dumb. We walk a little farther, pass another couple of men pulling telephone wires out of a backpack. "What?" I finally ask. She stops. "In a cave," she says slowly, "always, always look back. Every few minutes, turn around. Nothing looks the same coming out as it did going in, so you have to memorize the backsides of every boulder, the shape of the hole you've just come through, see the reverse of every angle of slope. You have to know how it should look going back out so you can tell if you're in the right passage." I tell myself I must remember her warning, train myself to turn around, take a series of mental snapshots I could click back through on my way out, matching what I remember from when I came in to what's in front of me as I head back out.

It's an act for which the gods would punish me. Their demands are clear: In the underworld, you're not allowed to look back. It was Orpheus' big mistake and he paid for it. When his bride Eurydice was bitten by a snake and died, Orpheus, inconsolable, ignored all advice and headed for the underworld to retrieve her. He was renowned for his music and took his lyre with him, intending to charm anything in

Hades that kept him from his love. And it worked. The guard dog Cerberus cocked his three heads at the sound and quit barking. Tantalus forgot his thirst, Sisyphus sat down on his stone, the wheel of Ixion quit turning. Even the stone walls of the passages softened, the Furies wept, and finally Hades appeared and granted Orpheus' wish on one condition: that as the two of them left the underworld they must not once look back.

How to understand Hades' dictate? I want it to be more than a simple taboo against reporting to others what the exit looked like and more than a simple test of obedience. Why would the gods not want you to look back? Parents do, teachers do, almost all authorities do; they reward the retrospective, the careful consideration of what's happened; they hope the past instructs. About our personal stories, we're urged to tell events exactly as they happened. In the therapist's office, memoir-writing groups, at family reunions, and with intimate friends, we're urged to turn back, shine a light on the past, tell it like it was. There's some healing, of course, in such recounting of our lives. And maybe some prevention. "Those who cannot remember the past," George Santayana reminds us, "are condemned to repeat it." Certainly in a cave, such looking back means you're less likely to get stuck down here; you're more likely to get out, leave the cave behind, emerge back into the fresh air of the present.

The underworld that Orpheus entered is not the literal cave, though, but the mythic cave, the cave as metaphor for the sunless caverns some of us sink to from time to time. The place we wander in sorrow, in depression, in aimlessness, the place Emily Dickinson describes as the "depths in every consciousness from which we cannot rescue ourselves—to which none can go with us." In such a cave, rescue is impossible, as is the carefully planned return. In such a cave, you can't go back the same way you came in. You move *through* the underworld. It's a passageway. You don't go in, look around, memorize certain stalagmites, certain boulders, and then when your trail mix runs low, think *okay, that's far enough,* retrace your steps, and come back out the entrance.

In a literal cave, you want certainty, the passages marked, a map, and three sources of light: backup batteries, carbide, extra bulbs. In a metaphorical cave, you go empty-handed. You enter ambiguity, the angst of too many passages, undiscovered exits, and the absence of light. You're lost in the dark, which is the whole point.

A successful trip in the literal cave most likely means you exit by the same route you entered. A successful trip in the metaphorical cave means you will not. For this reason, the backward glance in the literal cave means survival, and in the metaphorical cave, it means failure: Orpheus turns around to make sure Eurydice is still there. The gods shake their heads and pull her back into the cave; Orpheus watches as she turns pale again, wraithlike, and disappears forever. He begs for another chance, but the gods refuse. His best love is lost and the rest of his days are full of grief and regret.

I've always loved Orpheus, the way his life is such testament to the power of music. But I wouldn't want him in a cave with me, wouldn't want a romantic who can't be practical, who can't separate the literal from the metaphorical. A romantic might charm the bats into deeper torpor, turn flashlights into candles he sets on a boulder with crackers and cheese, spread his overalls across underground streams so that you can keep your feet dry. For the romantic, the cave becomes scenery, the set designed for the play of imagination. He won't realize he's wasting light or risking hypothermia. Or maybe he'd think it was worth it. I've done a little of both myself, sat enchanted against a cave wall, letting my light play over the boulders until conduction chilled my backside and the beam began to flicker. The trouble with a romantic is that he can get you killed—gloriously, perhaps, but killed nevertheless. Or if you manage to escape, that after the initial enchantment he'll be disappointed in everything else. Maybe Orpheus' mistake, in fact, was not just the result of confusing the literal with the metaphorical. Maybe Orpheus deliberately turned around. Maybe he knew no long-term marriage could live up to its early romance. Maybe he decided against a life with Eurydice, the tedium of morning tea and milking goats, and chose, instead, a life of lament and then high-drama death at the hands of the limb-rending Maenads.

"Right," Emily says, "no romantics in the cave. And no showoffs either. In a cave they're a pain in the ass." They show off, she says, want to be the fastest climber or crawler. Glory-hogs, they take unnecessary risks and put the rest of the team in danger. Even the cleverest needs the others. Odysseus got his men out of the Cyclops' cave only because the sheep cooperated, didn't buck or bleat as his men fastened themselves to their underbellies and rode out undetected by the blind monster who sat at the entrance feeling the tops of their woolly heads.

Nor would I want to go caving with someone too brave, not wary enough of danger. Floyd Collins, the famous caver trapped in a Kentucky cave for two weeks, made two mistakes: He went in alone and he told no one where he was headed. But he was experienced, he must have reasoned to himself, one of the best in the country. He squeezed through seventy feet and, too confident, kept going on and on to the one place where not one of us has any experience at all.

"Turn around," Emily reminds me now that we're underground. "Keep looking back." We'd passed a dozen men and women huddled in small groups near the cave's entrance, some with maps, others with walkie-talkies, canteens, first-aid kits. Emily had fastened me into a seat harness and lowered me down the twenty-foot drop to the cave floor. She'd reached between my legs to unfasten things and I was reminded again how irrelevant dignity is in a cave. No romance, no heroics, no prudishness. Now, as I turn my head and study where we've just come from, she fastens a pink ribbon to my coveralls to indicate to the team practicing the rescue that I'm not a player, not a victim, not a supervisor. A rock, she tells me. The ribbon means I'm a rock. Nobody's going to pay any attention to me. We're about to head deeper into the cave, toward the Gun Barrel. She has a half-hour or so before she has to supervise the mock rescue of a man who has mock-broken a bone way back in one of the side passages of the cave. I'm pleased by my designation, the way the ribbon makes me invisible, and then, no, I remind myself, the ribbon is symbolic and I'm in a literal cave, and though there's no chance of getting lost here, I'd do well to practice the backward glance.

I do. There, in the beam of my flashlight, are the ropes, even a shaky old ladder, enough markers that I, returning from deeper in the cave, could find this place again and the way out. And not only backwards, Emily reminds me, but up. Memorize the ceiling, she says, where it lowers and flattens, where it soars or chunks. Above me, forty or fifty feet above me, the stone walls lean in and converge in what looks like an upside-down bowl. A dome, Emily calls it, conjuring images of Coleridge's Kubla Khan and his pleasure dome. I'm standing below a pleasure dome, only it seems too small to be called a dome, more like a well, and I'm in the bottom. Somewhere up there in the pocked wall is the lip I backed over in a seat harness ten minutes ago, and somewhere back beyond that, the men with their maps, and from somewhere else Coleridge's later lines: "through caverns measureless to man / Down to a sunless sea," this scene without ropes or ladder, without Emily, without the forty-five people outside getting ready to practice a rescue, without pleasure. Baby Jessica. Tighter walls, much tighter, twenty-two feet down in a well in Midland, Texas. Eighteen months old. I remember the pictures, try to imagine how the world must have looked to her, surrounded by dark, as she looked up at the helmeted men leaning over the opening above, calling down to her, asking her about the sound a kitten makes, anything to bring some normalcy to the bottom of a pit that squeezed too close, too stony-hard, pinning her down there for three days.

I watched television for hours, mesmerized by her plight, her parents' panic, the rescuers' dogged resolve, and by the irresistible urge to imagine myself down there. Something about that predicament draws the imagination in a way no similar plight does. Climbers get caught on high cliffs in Yosemite, on mountaintops in the Cascades, hikers get lost in the Alaskan wilderness, sailors at sea, but I don't put myself in their places the way I do with a person caught in a cleft belowground. Maybe to be stranded on a high ridge or lost in the vast sea or wilderness has something of glory to help mediate the despair. Panoramic vision, the odyssey of it all, invites a larger context, the landscape of wide history and myth, the wilderness cry one can imagine a god wanting to answer. The guy caught in the cave has none of that. It's dark. Nobody can see him, and he can't see anybody. Vision's impossible. He's trapped in a small crack, a nameless bug in the stone. Maybe he can wave an arm in the dark, maybe wiggle a foot.

When I was ten or eleven, I was obsessed with short stories about being buried alive. Poe's "The Cask of Amontillado," "The Black Cat," "The Pit and the Pendulum," "The Premature Burial." I read about Pompeii, people entombed in lava and ash, about the sacrificial burials of living children in ancient cultures. I'd lie upstairs on my yellow gingham bedspread on summer late afternoons and imagine the last brick put in place, the pendulum dropping closer, the walls closing in, dirt clods on my face, my body thrashing inside a wooden box, my small hands moving frantically under the softness of ash. And then the fatigue of so much effort, the dry mouth, muscles weakening by the day. Such an ignoble way to die. And so slowly. Not the sudden fall, but the slow diminishment, the eyes-open, see-nothing wasting away.

I'd imagine, too, the rescuers nearby, perhaps within ear-shot, but unable to break through or unwilling to risk a dangerous rescue. At what point do they stop drilling, shoveling, feeding oxygen lines down to the trapped? How do you tell someone who's alive and well, but trapped, that you can't reach him? That there's nothing more you can do? Several years ago I had a cat who got trapped between the ceiling in my basement and the main floor. I'd had some work done in the kitchen; the carpenter had pulled a panel away from one section of wall and exposed a small access to the adjacent bathroom plumbing, access that opened up for the cat a whole world between the two floors. A world of joists and mice. It took a couple of days before I realized she wasn't just avoiding the carpenter by hiding in the basement. The hole had been closed, the stove shoved back into place. She was an indoor cat and at first I feared the worst: that the workers had left an exterior door open too long, that she'd disappeared into surrounding acres of owl beaks and bobcats. About ten o'clock on the second night, I heard her. I went outside. I came back in, heard her again, finally realized what had happened, and knew I couldn't move the stove myself and couldn't sleep knowing she was trapped in a six-inch space just below my feet. My grown daughter's bedroom is in the basement. Her walls are still covered with prom pictures, the bureau with pom-poms. The cat was caught in her ceiling. I dragged a stepladder across the carpet, climbed up with a hammer in my hand, and slammed it up, made a dimple in the drywall, slammed harder and then harder, the dimple denting and then cracking and the drywall crumbling and finally a hole I could reach my hand into, only to realize she wasn't caught between these two joists, but between two others somewhere nearby, and I moved the stepladder two feet to the right, climbed up and bashed another hole and then another and another, the stuffed bears in the room now littered with plaster bits and of course all the noise terrified the cat who had by now slunk as far from me as the joists would allow and would not come, not even when I wormed my hand up in the space, lured her with kiddlebits and all the dumb *here kitty-kitties* I could think of. An hour went by, more holes, more pleading; I couldn't bear her thinking I'd given up and gone to bed, that I'd crossed the line between not-quitting and quitting. Make sure she hears you, I kept saying to myself, bang and call and rattle the cat food, make sure she knows you're trying. Keep her from whatever cat form of despair she might feel. I would have destroyed the whole room to get her out.

I don't know if cats experience hope; I do know that's what I couldn't let her lose. Or maybe it was my own hope that I couldn't bear losing. And yet ahead there must be for all of us a moment of resignation when the body instructs the mind about the inevitable. Heroes, perhaps, are those who hold out longer than most, who give themselves another chance. I admire such ferocity. Or is it stubbornness? All I know is that it's easier to be brave for the helpless than it is for myself.

I think about the philosophy student again, wonder how he'd occupied his mind. And Floyd Collins—what did he think about for fifteen days? Pinned in a crack by a fallen rock, he endured the first twenty-four hours in that Kentucky cave alone in the dark. When friends found him, they freed his upper body, but could not budge the rock that had fallen and wedged his lower body. They brought lanterns and water, a little food. Then the cave grew unstable and the rescuers grew afraid and finally they withdrew. For two weeks, Collins languished, just 120 feet from the entrance, less than half a football field, stuck feet-first in a small crevice that tightened around him the more he wriggled to free himself while the press gathered topside along with thousands of others, some keeping a vigil, others just gawking, selling souvenirs, a few preaching fire and brimstone. In there alone for fifteen days, Collins finally died.

If I thought at all about my childhood obsession back then, I might have thought it had to do with the titillation of being safely scared, an unmolested voyeur of terror enlivened by what I, secure on the sidelines, had avoided. Maybe that's why I go into caves—because of an overarching fear of safe dullness, my own moments of dullness especially, which unnerve me. I've long had a need to resist the slide from tranquil to doltish. Inertia's a powerful force, and toward the people in my life—teachers, writers, lovers, friends—who've rescued me from its lethargy, I feel enormous appreciation. I've thanked them, of course, even as I've also wished I'd been known for a streak of wildness so that the tenderness of my gratitude might seem all the more unexpected. Such uncharacteristic gestures can seem especially poignant, as a story about a raccoon reminded me.

A man I barely knew told me what happened. He had just rappelled down to the bottom of a dry cave and was about to step off rope when something suddenly grabbed his pant leg. Hearing his screams, the rest of the team, still topside, hauled him up quickly. When he swung his leg up over the lip, they found an emaciated raccoon, its teeth sunk into the man's flesh. The coon had evidently fallen into the cave some time ago. Unable to crawl out or to find food where it was, it had grown scrawny and weak, though not so much so that it couldn't recognize a rescue. Its fur hung down, even dragged on the ground. The cavers managed to pry it loose, offered it cookies from their backpacks, and finally rappelled back into the cave to resume their exploration. When they emerged hours later, the raccoon was still there, weakened further by diarrhea prompted by the cookies. In a gesture I understand, it managed to crawl over to its rescuer and put its head on the toe of his boot.

Emily tells me about her own rescue from a cave several years ago. She'd fallen, broken a kneecap, and had to be carried out miles underground on a stretcher. I'd read about that rescue, an extraordinary ordeal involving 170 volunteers, a skilled caver strapped flat on a stretcher, pushed through the same torturous wormholes, carried over rifts, hauled up drop-offs she'd managed skillfully on the way in, three and a half days of pain-jerking carryout. "Did you ever want to give up, stay where you were?" She just looks at me, and I remember how the press, reporting her spirits at the end, broadcast her requests for pizza and a margarita. I decide that if I ever get trapped in a cave, I want someone like Emily with me. Practical, skilled, no-nonsense. Someone who won't play games, who knows her own fears and mine, and is sure of the reasons for getting out.

Emily finally leads me to the far corner of a small room and points with her light to a small crawlway we have to scoot through. "The Gun Barrel's on the other side of that," she says. For some reason, she loves the Gun Barrel, wants to show it to me, the way one might show a friend a new sculpture or dress. I'm down on my hands and knees, ready to duck my head under when suddenly I can't do it. Can't do it at all. I back out. I'm not panicky this time, just clear. I tell her I can't. I can't believe I'm saying this; she's one of the world's foremost cave rescue people; she's handled panic and foolishness and accidents and long ordeals underground, and I'm telling her I can't go through a short crawlway to see something she wants me to see. Something's inserted itself in my mind, set up a barrier, blocked off everything but this refusal. Orpheus' underworld, Odysseus' or Baby Jessica's travails? This isn't *like* anything else. It is what it is: a cave, darkness, a tight squeeze. I back away more, and my mind flashes to Jeanne and I know she's too far gone.

"But I'm right here; I'll be right next to you," Emily offers. I hate my reaction, but that doesn't change it. I stand up and apologize. She shrugs and waits a few quiet moments and then, when I don't waver, says she wants me to test the backward glances I'd practiced on the way in. Which way? she asks, encouraging me to take the initial step. I try to clear my head. With my back to the crawl-through, I think I recognize the first boulder and guess we should go left. But I'm not sure, and then I don't recognize a thing, have no idea which way to go. A couple of guys approach, laying temporary telephone lines and rope for rigging, rope for hauling out a stretcher with a pretend victim.

I ask Emily about the philosophy student, what he did to keep his hopes up. "He decided to think about three things," she begins, watching the trainees maneuver their equipment around a corner, "and only three things. First, to stay warm. Second, to keep circulation moving in his leg. And third, to believe he'd get out. If any other thought came into his mind, he threw it out."

No speculating, no supposing, and no panic. Utterly fo-
cused. Clear-minded. Which is not, I realize, what I've been
for the last hour in the cave, talking with Emily, trying to
memorize landmarks while I thought about Baby Jessica,
Floyd Collins, even Orpheus. Knowing Emily would keep
me from danger, I became exactly the caving companion I
wouldn't want to be with—musing and distracted, my mind
drifting to metaphor and death. No wonder I couldn't go
through the squeeze. I'd been thinking about all the wrong
things.

Is that why Jeanne has begun to send us all away? Does
she feel as if she's in her own version of a squeeze, so far into
the realm of no return that she might require a clear-minded-
ness about death? Through years of illness, I admired what
sustained her—bravery and determination, her reliance on
friends—and now I'm struck by what she doesn't want anymore: no romantics, nor he words of the blustery cocksure.
And no one along who's too inclined to metaphor and myth,
those attempts to attach wider context to an experience that
must seem to her now more and more narrow, tapering to
constriction. Jeanne's almost out of reach, and I'm at a stop-
ping point, a woman afraid, a woman with a pink ribbon sig-
nifying nothing.

DARK WINGS TO ZERO

Under every deep a lower deep opens.

— RALPH WALDO EMERSON

MY FRIEND LIZ did her master's thesis on bat shit. She spread mist nets across some caves in western Maryland and then carefully removed the bats that got tangled there, put them in Styrofoam cups, where they obligingly deposited their feces, which won them their release. Back in the lab, she dried the feces in aluminum foil cups and stored them in glass vials. Just before she examined them under a microscope, she softened them and teased apart the pellets with a pin stuck in the needle of a syringe. She spent a lot of time in caves and with bats and their shit. Why? I asked her. The official answer: She was investigating the feeding habits of these bats, analyzing differences within and among the four cave-dwelling species common in the area. The unofficial answer: She likes them.

Jim tells me we should see bats today, eastern pipistrelles, most likely. Pips, he's calls them, as if he's talking about small dogs. It's late summer; five of us are hiking up the hill in western Maryland toward the same cave where I, ten years ago, had taken my young students, the same cave at which I'd panicked, been unable to enter. Jim knows nothing of that experience and I'm pretty sure I've done enough caving by now that I don't need to tell him or any of the others. The cave is on Nature Conservancy property, protected by a high fence and a gate, which Jim unlocks. In the center of the fenced-in area is the pit and at the bottom of the pit, I know, is the low-ceilinged, downward-slanting entrance to the cave itself. I don't look at it. Maybe I'm thinking if I don't really see the hole, I'll feel no fear this time and I'll get through it and into the cave itself with no problem. Maybe if I picture, instead of the opening itself, Liz in her boots, stretching her nets here, snagging creatures used to flying freely in and out, I can do it. We scramble down the pit and, as before, ten years ago, the others enter the opening ahead of me, sliding on their stomachs headfirst, and finally I crouch down and look at it, a fairly unjumbled entrance. And then, as before, ten years ago, I feel it again: I'm about to be swallowed. I stand up, trying to fight off the black curtain of panic that's the only possible response to the fear that I'm about to disappear, only it's not a body, a cave, the earth, about to consume me. I don't understand this, but here's how it feels: What I'm going into is the opposite. It's nothingness. I'm about to wiggle down a chute, pebbles under my chin, mud slick on my belly, then slide faster and faster and at the bottom isn't dirt or stone but nothingness, the world drops away, I'll fall out of a stone cockpit, only it won't be familiar sky I'll fall through, not the earth I'll be falling toward, not the ordinary green and brown of the land, but black fog or an empty galaxy, and if I go through that hole I'm a goner, a cave astronaut without a tether.

I look away. Deep breaths, deep breaths. What is it about *this* cave entrance? I've heard Liz describe the bats here, I've studied the map of this cave, heard Jim outline the passages, what's first, what's next. Of course I know there's something very concrete beyond this entrance. I tell myself I *will* do this and suddenly Jim materializes behind me, and he's looking at me, and I don't say anything, I just do it. I get down and start wiggling in. I make myself look at the cave walls, whatever's near me. I grab a small twig, remnant of an inwashed branch, reminder of a tree, and keep it in my hand. I keep scooching down and in, farther and farther; I twist my head and look behind me and here comes Jim, who loves this, and in less than a minute I'm all the way in and it's over.

The chute ends on a small ledge. Twelve feet below me is the main cave passage, the beautiful wet cave, utterly solid and stony, full of juts and jags, plenty of rough edges to keep me firmly here, placing a foot, a hand, a hip carefully, paying for any slip of attention, not with free-fall through outer space but with a bruise. The upper world vanishes, along with the images of galaxies. I move out of Jim's way, let him get in the lead.

Within a few minutes we're figuring out how to navigate the tight, contorting drop down to the main floor. He coaches us through, telling us to turn one hip or the other, to get the left foot ready, to let go as we twist our torsos and squeeze down and through and then there's another ledge and the left foot's on it, and I jump down and the rest of the cave lies easily ahead. One of the other women gets stuck. Her chest is too big, she complains. Jim reassures her, tells her to let all the air out of her lungs and finally she's through and drops carefully down to the cave floor, joking about the Appalachian cave method of breast reduction. Her humor relieves us all.

This is a crevice cave, a narrow, two-to-five-foot-wide slit in the limestone through which a small stream runs. We walk and try to keep our feet out of the water, walk and rock-hop and shine our lights on the walls. They're high, buff-colored, and beautiful. I feel as if I've been dropped inside the high dunes of Cape Cod, the sand wind-whipped and petrified into stone. Or sent inside a sand painting's layers of copper and tan. Above us, a many-ton ceiling of stone blocks out all light. It's cool and damp and I feel both relief and trepidation to have made it through what nobody here knows had so terrorized me years ago, to be moving now through a dark fissure thirty feet below the surface of the earth. Above me, the trees push down their roots; the grass is a late-summer green in the heat. Down here, Jim was right about seeing bats.

Most people don't like them. They look like some botched experiment, their scrunched, almost-human faces, their absurdly big ears, the misshapen nose and leathery wings. They belong to the order of mammals Chiroptera, meaning "wing-handed." They fly with their hands. Early Latin writers associated the bat with the devil, and medieval artists depicted Satan with batlike wings. I actually like their comic looks and I know their contributions—they devour mosquitoes and pollinate fruits, to name just two. I love to watch them high up in the summer evening skies, the sudden twists and plunges of their flights that look more like kite than bird, the steep banks and aerobatics. You can almost imagine them with bright colors and string, with a human on the ground holding on, running through a field, controlling the flight. Only there's no nylon up there in the wind, just pinched little bat faces, mouths full of teeth, large ears, and fleshy forearms. And there's no sky in here where the bats cling to the walls just a few feet from my head.

The bat shit Liz studied is crucial. Bats are one of the primary transporters of organic material from the upper world to the lower. Biologists estimate that in the South, a hundred million bats devour more than a hundred thousand tons of insects annually, which means thousands of tons of insect-laced bat feces deposited inside caves. Rich, organic feces, high in phosphorus and soaked with nitrogen-rich bat urine. The cave crickets and beetles, worms and millipedes, lice and ticks fight over the fresh stuff. Microorganisms attack it. Fungi bloom on it, turn a dollop into what looks like the seedy head of a dandelion. Without it, the cave community would starve.

So might surrounding communities. In Texas, New Mexico, in Brazil, Borneo, and Egypt, where tons of guano accumulate in piles that can be a hundred feet deep, a kind of mounded, feces-swamp way back in a cave, local people wade in with shovels. They scoop and lift and trudge out with bags of shit on their backs. They use it for fertilizer. Small guano-mining operations continue in many caves today. But this cave is too small for heaps of guano. Small droppings might be underfoot, stuck now in the treads of my boots, but there's no ammonia odor here, no black mass to wade through, just the clear stream to try to stay out of and the occasional dozing bat.

Far below the light of the cave entrance, I think about Plato, wonder what it would mean if his myth were reversed. How might Western thinking have evolved differently if the man who broke his chains in the cave looked up toward the light but changed his mind, pivoted, went down instead, farther into the cave, deeper than the fire, down to where there's no light at all, beyond shadows where even the body seems to fade? What kind of knowledge might he bring back? What would it mean to be *endarkened*?

We keep going back and back. After the entrance, it's one

of the relatively undemanding caves you can walk and day-dream in at the same time, without worrying about falling into abysses. There are only a few passages here that are so skinny you have to turn your body, sidle through. The others walk and talk and maybe they're thinking about other things too, salamanders or dinner or the ache in their neck. Rock ledges jut out into the crevice above our heads. They're like high closet shelves, sometimes straight, sometimes scalloped. Jim occasionally stops us, shines his light up into a high dome, and later leads us over to a small waterfall that cascades out of the ceiling and runs down the wall. I think of Tantalus, doomed to spend eternity in Hades with an unquenchable thirst for water that is always just out of reach. *Tantalized?* Not me. I climb over and put my hands in the cold, clear stream.

Jim points out a few more bats, flitting high up near the ceiling. They're small, a few inches long, brown and furry. They look like gerbils. When they sleep, they hang upside down, a position no one can completely explain. Some biologists think the stance reduces bats' vulnerability to predators or that it's easier to take off in flight if they start from an upside-down position. Some artists pictured them enacting the old Satan stories. They're looking down, they're headed to the underworld, their wings darkened into wings of fear, of death. A photograph unblurs in my head: a spear-nosed bat that's been tranquilized and placed on its back. Its wings—seventeen inches of black leather—are spread wide and pinned down to the lab table. Its toes are long, clawlike. It looks crucified. One eye appears to be open.

I'm alone again in the cave. The others have headed back. I want a few minutes by myself, I'd told Jim, but the truth is I'm not sure what I want.

Jeanne has died. Her husband had called a few nights ago

to tell me she'd slipped into a coma. No, he said, don't come. "Can she hear you talk to her?" I asked him. He didn't know. I wanted her to not be afraid but I didn't know why she should or shouldn't be. I had no idea where she was, what goes on at the end. He called again in the morning.

Bat shit, bat stories. The things with which we distract ourselves. The cave drips all around me. I feel the way I did the last time I saw her, when we'd sat in silence, when I couldn't think of anything to say and she seemed beyond words anyway, and I'd felt as if some great thing turned its face, began to lumber away.

If I stay utterly still, there's only silence interrupted by drips. I'd liken the sound to tears, but it's not sadness I feel, nothing as pointed as the grief of her dying. It's bigger, the sound of the mountain wearing away, the sound of erasure, of going, going, gone. It drips into this underground space, it drips beside my head, onto my right arm, it hollows stone away.

I feel oddly close to her here. I want to say she feels nearby, but that's not it. It's absence that feels nearby, and it neither comforts nor scares. For the moment it seems that the people, the trees, the fluttering bats—they're all some illusion, a delusion perhaps, a way of avoiding the truth that nothingness permeates everything, nestles inside the heart of it all. Seventy-five percent of the universe, some scientists say, seems to be made of nothing. Dark matter, they call it, shadow matter, wimpzillas. This cave feels full of it, an almost visceral dark matter I want to lie down with.

The lives of bats include long, built-in pauses, time to slow down while the world continues above them, without them. I don't want dormancy or coma. I want the quiet of a long, undisturbed lull. I take off my helmet and lean my bare head back to rest against the damp wall.

When the composer John Cage wrote a piece in the 1960s entitled 4'33", audiences didn't know how to react. Some grumbled, some actually stormed the stage. Some left. The piece begins when the pianist sits down at the piano. He sits there. A minute or so goes by and he lowers and raises the lid of the piano, another couple of minutes, another lowering and raising. He sits there. The silence gets very loud. You begin to hear people's bodies shifting in their seats, you hear their breath, the small noises in their mouths. Another minute goes by. And then thirty-three seconds more. And then he gets up and bows and exits the stage. It gets referred to as the "silent piece." But of course it's not silent. What people first listen to is each other, the guy behind them fidgeting, the foot over there tapping, somebody's clothing rustling, the sounds of impatience and settling down, and finally they end up listening to themselves, the unspoken questions, then the unspoken, then the blood in their ears, the sound of their own breath, the quiet, the less quiet, and the more.

I want to imagine Plato's man-in-the-cave coming down here, down to this realm. I want to imagine him showing me other bits of wisdom, something akin to what Yeats had in mind when he said: "I shall find the dark grow luminous, the void fruitful when I understand I have nothing." I listen again to the dripping. It never, ever stops. I don't know if that's consolation or torture.

My nose is cold. My backside's cold. I can see my breath. I get up and follow the stream back toward the entrance. Sunlight filters down into the twilight zone. I feel it on my skin. I twist and clamber up the jagged drop and wriggle up the slanted entrance that has its history of frightening me and out the hole to the bottom of the pit, where I pause. The others have already climbed all the way out, are up in full sun again, removing their helmets, taking swigs of water. I turn around and look back at the entrance. It's an opening into small carved-out-of-stone passages; it's a chute to an enormous other world. We go back and forth between light and dark, reason and passion—I could go on and on. If Plato's man goes farther down first, and then up, would he know, better than I do, if he's coming back out of something large or something small? Would any of us recognize what he brings back, know whether it's merely mud on his face or a bit of bat shit, or something else? What if he came back silent?

Above me, Jim grabs my hand and helps me up the last few feet of the pit. "Good," he smiles. I can't tell what he's praising. Or maybe he's just glad I'm safely back up to the surface.

What is it I want? Or need? To consider the possibility that what's tucked in these inner pockets is nothing, the risk that it's everything, the danger that it's both, and that it's one of my jobs to discover the difference. That maybe one way to keep nothingness from turning into despair is to pay attention, as best one can, to what's unseen. Is that what *endarkened* means? I think of Robert Frost, leaning over the deep well, looking down and more down and, just once, through his reflection, seeing it: "something white, uncertain, / Something more of the depths . . . Truth? A pebble of quartz?" he asks.

Maybe just the bats, whose bodies will be glistening in a few months, the cave's moisture beading on their fur while they hang torpid all winter long, waiting for warmth. Their heartbeats will have slowed to five beats a minute. Their body temperature will have plummeted to just above freezing. Their breaths will come slowly, only seven or eight times a minute in a state deeper than sleep. They'll cling upside down to the cave ceiling and the water will drip past their folded wings, their barely rising chests, their toothed mouths, closed eyes, giant ears. If they opened an eye, the drip might look to them like water rising out of the earth, a slow fountain falling up.

12

IN THE HOLLOW THAT REMAINS

Go inside a stone.
That would be my way.

— CHARLES SIMIC

And the sublime comes down
To the spirit itself,
The spirit and space,
The empty spirit
In vacant space.

— WALLACE STEVENS

A FEW MONTHS LATER, on a gray December day, I was
squeezed into a cleft in 350-million-year-old limestone, trying to remember the final lines of Charles Simic's poem. Just
an inch from my nose, a small circle of wet rock glowed
in the light of my headlamp. Above me, the fissure nar-
rowed into darkness. I felt as if I were inside a gash whose
skin at the top had healed over, sealing me in at the bottom. I
could swing my light up, watch its small beam skim over
ancient walls, wrinkled and creased, like ocher-brown mus-

cle turned to stone. Here at the bottom, I kept my body turned sideways in the cleft, shoulder blades pressed against the back wall. To move, I had to slide one foot slowly to the left, shift my weight to it, bring the other foot along, resist the urge to turn ninety degrees and stride ahead, an urge that, if heeded, could get me seriously wedged in stone sixty feet under the earth, two thousand feet away from the cave entrance. I took a deep breath, felt my upper body expand against the walls in front of and behind me and inched along, remembering that I love Simic's poem because it asks me to imagine space inside an object I'd thought of as only solid, impenetrable.

Two hours into those limestone fissures, exhausted, I pulled out the map and saw that no matter where in the cave they went, the guide and other clients on this wild-cave tour would have to retrace their steps and come back through this small room again. I could stay here and rejoin them on the return trek. This wish to sit by myself had nothing to do with any self-imposed trial, no testing my tolerance of dark solitude. I just needed to rest, needed the stillness of sitting and not fretting over where to place my foot, my fingers, how to clamber up and over a boulder I could see only in fragmented light as I swung my headlamp over it. The guide hesitated and then agreed and the group disappeared down a passageway. I sat down, leaned against a stone wall, took a deep breath, and turned off my lamp.

There was absolutely no light. Every time, it's a state that needs testing. You squint, hold your hands up to your face, wait for your pupils to dilate. Nothing happens. No glimmer, no pale outlines, no softening of a darkness so palpable you feel as if you ought to be able to wring it, wrest from it a beam or two of light. Total blackness. You wave your hand in nothingness, sure your fingers are setting off ripples of darkness, that your hands are leaving behind them a V-shaped wake of the less-dark. Without landmarks or skymarks, you begin to lose your bearings. You pick up a rock, consider hurling it toward the last wall you saw, consider how you'll feel if it doesn't thunk, but instead sails noiselessly and forever through the silence of an abyss at whose edge your backpack teeters, how it could be you're not halfway between Millstream Passage and Sleepy Rock at all, but somewhere else equally immense, sunless, moonless. You put down the rock.

I wish I could say that silent darkness moved me to some instant insight. That I suddenly understood why Buddhists prize emptiness. But what mattered was that I got to rest and nothing dramatic happened. The memory of my previous terror, the decade-ago vision of my cousin's death, brushed faintly through me and triggered an almost imperceptible moment of anxiety. I flipped my light on, looked around, turned it off again. Stillness. It was as if those events had happened to another me. It became, in fact, oddly peaceful in that niche two thousand feet inside a limestone mountain. I became very conscious of invisible space, room to feel Jeanne's death again, and my father's. Still. And more deeply. The limestone cracks gouged out by acidic water so many millions of years ago, the cavern walls inching back, the stone hollowed out. And some space in me opening up, what happens, perhaps, when fear and sorrow unclench their fists, uncurl their fingers, open the palms wide. Room. An underground recess full of nothing.

Until footsteps and a small light approached and a voice in the dark said he too needed to rest and did I mind? Though he was apparently one of the group and, like me, too tired to continue, I couldn't picture which man this was. The one in khaki overalls? The guy with wire-rimmed glasses? I saw his tiny beam go off, heard him drop his pack, settle himself on the cave floor. For a few minutes neither of us said a thing. And then, with no introduction, he told me he'd once been frozen to the deck of a Navy ship in the early sixties, that they'd had to chip the Arctic ice from around his body, that he'd permanently lost all feeling in his right nostril. From there to his various jobs, the vagaries of his long marriage, the indulgences and difficulties, gestures of courage or supplication.

"I'm with my son on this trip," he told me; "we used to cave together often. Maybe this'll be good for us." His voice was soft, with none of the guilt of confession or the neediness of bravado. It didn't feel so much as if he were unburdening himself, hauling secrets out of deep hiding, sharing them, trembly-voiced, with a stranger he knew he'd never see. It was more as if I were sitting inside his secrets. And then he inside mine, my small moments of bravery and shame, romances and loss, job disappointments and griefs, the time when I, disillusioned by college, lied to my parents and left campus to ride a bus for ten days with only clean underwear and a few dollars in my pocket. It was more than the ease of talking to a stranger in the dark. It was as if the fissures and folds of our minds had slipped outside, become a part of the cave's cool interior, a place where we both could talk and listen carefully. Something about all that invisible space elicited an interaction that lacked agenda or charge, until finally even the very personal became, oddly, neither his nor mine, became simply the acknowledgment of human foibles and the occasional thought: *Ah, that too.*

In spite of the weight of some things we said, there was nothing weighty about anything we said, nothing intense about our conversation. The drama of our lives grew lighter, became no big deal. Picture a watercolorist diluting an intense indigo sky, adding water, more water. The sky lightens, fades from deep blue to pale blue, gets larger and more open, less threatening. Our words floated out into the dark and disappeared. On and on we went, the tedium of trivia and fatigue, of fear, his despair the day they diagnosed Parkinson's disease, the pain of my habitual reserve.

I surprised myself. I'm usually fairly private, certainly vigilant about solitude, famous—or infamous—among my friends for protecting my time alone. Selfish even. And yet there I was sixty feet below the earth's surface, my intention to settle into the great stillness of a cave broken by an invisible stranger with whom I sat, cross-legged and contented. The minutes, the half-hours, slipped by. We kept talking. He said he could see my aura. Imagine it? I asked. No, *see* it, he said. It was pitch-black in there. In other circumstances, I might have grown skeptical, bored, irritated at his intrusion, chagrined by my own admissions. But inside the stone fissure, those usual, easy reactions seemed to evaporate, dissolve in the darkness. It wasn't apathy or indifference I felt but, curiously, a *dis*passionate interest in what we were saying. There seemed to be plenty of time, an eternity, in fact. And a growing awareness of tremendous room. This is the irony that, in retrospect, I find most compelling: that it was spaciousness, not claustrophobia, that I felt inside that stone cave. And that the spaciousness was not just physical but psychic as well.

There's a Tibetan word, *shul*, meaning the hollow that remains after something has moved through. Buddhist monks use the word to refer to the path of emptiness, the way that opens up when one stops clinging to dogma. In Yiddish, *shul* means temple, a place to pray and to learn. Was there something about that ancient, mostly undisturbed space, that *shul*, that made such largess, such generous attentiveness, possible?

The man and I were anonymous, invisible to each other,

almost disembodied. The only sense we had of the other's place in the world, what position, status, what class we usually occupied, was rudimentary. We knew only that we happened to be in that cave at the same time. Everything else seemed interesting but mildly irrelevant, as if such a space unnamed us, made us any two humans paused within the normal pleasures and troubles of their lives.

A few weeks earlier I'd attended the annual conference of the National Speleological Society, wandered around a huge parking lot full of vehicles with bat bumper stickers, had coffee with some cavers. I'd asked a group of them what the draw was. Why crawl into such dark places? It's the great equalizer, they told me. Only one thing matters in there, and it's not your job, not your looks which nobody can see anyway, not your degrees or the speed of your Internet access. Everybody enters a cave dressed in rough overalls and hardhats, boots with good tread and gloves. You can study the others, try to get a sense of body shape and maybe age by limberness or lack of it. But that's about it. You could be inching on your behind down scrabbly slope in the mostly-dark next to the Queen of England and you'd never know it. The only thing that matters in a cave, they told me, is your ability to stay calm in dark spaces.

Later that afternoon, standing in the convention's art gallery, I studied a drawing titled "Cave Beneath Mt. Virgin." It's dark in that cave, too, except for a section of interior wall, which the artist had stippled platinum and pearl, a band of luminosity above a woman who stretches, naked, on the cave floor. The edge of her body glows orange. A woman stood next to me, both of us admiring the work. "Are you a caver?" I asked. "Yes," she answered. I asked her why and she told me a story about her addictions to drugs and alcohol, and about a friend who'd been killed in a cave. She'd felt such despair and such anger—why would anyone risk his life rappelling into the utter blackness of a sixty-foot well in old rock? His death compelled her to make her first trip into a cave in England. It turned her life around, she said. Instantly. I looked at her. Something about going into all that darkness, she struggled to explain. I'd heard cavers insist that anyone who's not comfortable in a cave is afraid of her own mind, that without the trappings and markers of our aboveground lives, the only thing left is the mind, and most of us aren't easy there. I told her about my own first cave terror. Perhaps it hadn't been claustrophobia or hallucinations at all, but a fear of empty space, the potential that absence holds, some inkling that those are inner spaces too. Robert Frost knew it: "I have it in me so much nearer home / To scare myself with my own desert places." The woman tried again to explain, but soon fell silent. Coffee was brewing on a table behind us; somebody was making change at the cash register. The question I really wanted to ask her was one I couldn't quite articulate, and even if I could, I knew she wouldn't be able to answer. I bought the drawing and left the gallery.

The ineffable, is, by definition, what words can't quite say. It's what silence is for. When we could hear the rest of the cavers returning, the man and I grew quiet. I heard him stand up, heard the rustle of nylon as he shouldered his pack. By the time the others' lights bounced off the walls and ceiling and their boots mingled with ours, he'd melted back into the group. I didn't look for him afterward, all of us out in the gray December day, unfastening our helmets and wiping the mud from our pants. It would have been wrong, a violation; the intimacy we'd had couldn't immediately be transported aboveground. Suddenly shy, I pulled up the hood of my sweatshirt and headed for my car.

Hearing this story later, a friend wondered if the man's coming back to sit with me had been motivated by something other than fatigue. A subtle flirtation? That hadn't even occurred to me. I'd had no sense of intent, felt none of the teasing or testing of seduction. Had I been too trusting? When all those markers that usually help determine our behaviors with another are absent, how do we gauge one another? What remains to guide us? At first, maybe nothing. Or fear of nothing. Maybe too much innocence. That last time, under Laurel Mountain, I wasn't afraid. Instead, it was as if that dark invisible cave-space invited the man and me to relax our boundaries, to expand.

I think again of the troglobites, permanent cave-dwellers, which have no need for color protection deep inside the earth, and are, therefore, often albino, almost transparent. Like the eyes of many cave creatures, those of the Kentucky cavefish have degenerated; the fish is blind. But its pale body is studded with vibration receptors, tiny sensors that can detect even a slow human hand dipping into the water. Ghostlike, the fish darts away. Cave crickets and beetles, a whole community of pale, blind creatures relying on extralong feelers, their sensitivity to one another's vibrations.

No, I told my friend, the man wasn't flirting. I may have been unable to see, may have been literally blind to his intentions, but my other senses were highly tuned and we were, for that brief time, not the parrying, sexual selves we so often bring to human interactions. Perhaps such space, hollowed-out and dark, a kind of rarified air, allows for presences more limpid, diaphanous, magnanimous, out of which emerge attentiveness, empathy, quiet voices, and highly tuned ears in a vast underground space.

What happened in there? I wondered later. Nothing, really. No terror, no startling revelations, no new friendship. A momentary connection with someone I'll never see again. And an unexpected sense of spaciousness. "Nothing happens?" the Spanish poet Juan Ramón Jiménez asks. "Or has everything happened, / and are we standing now, quietly, in the new life?"

Though for me it was an actual cave, a fissure in ancient stone, that precipitated that sense of spaciousness, that's not the only way to become aware of it. Loss can do it too, hollow you out, leave you, like an old stone, riddled with invisible caverns. Jeanne died, my father, others. The only ghost I've ever seen came in the shape of a dog. A week earlier, another good friend had died, unexpectedly. There were things we'd needed to say to each other and hadn't. The streets and stores were already decked out with holiday pizzazz, everywhere the flush of plenty, and inside me, again, this stunned silence, a saber-shaped absence I felt in my body as danger, grief like a weapon I could wound myself with if I moved too fast in any direction. The atmosphere thins in sorrow time. Things that had seemed centrally important a week earlier floated once more toward my peripheral vision and disappeared. Everything seemed suddenly fragile, less solid.

A week after my friend's funeral I woke in the middle of the night to hear chains rattling outside. From the window, I saw an alabaster blur circling the lilac tree at the corner of the field. I pulled on boots and went outside. The moon was full, the night sky bright with stars, the ground frozen under a foot of snow. A still night of silver and shadows and a pure white dog, his chain wrapped and wrapped around the base of the lilac.

I live in the woods, miles from town, and I know the two dogs who occasionally stop by on their treks along this ridge. I'd never seen this one before. He stood, neck trussed tight to the tree, and wagged his tail. I let him smell my palm and then I took his collar and we walked slowly around and around the tree, unwinding the chain. I was half asleep, not thinking about anything. I held on to him and walked in circles, each one a little wider than the last. Three times around, four. And then I wanted to keep going, to keep unwrapping his by-now-unwrapped chain, let him keep expanding the circle, making the orbit larger and wider, tracing an invisible, elliptical path through the woods, across the cornfields, down into the valley, back up through the woods, each orbit more far-flying than the last, the moon circling overhead, a dog at the end of a tether that grew longer and longer until he'd take off, some kind of airborne ghost-dog that would keep tugging the circumference of grief outward.

My boots crunched in the moonlit snow as I removed the chain. Untangled, the dog hesitated. And then he turned and loped across the yard, into the woods and was gone.

I've never seen him since. How to explain all this? It was an actual dog. I went out in the morning and looked at his paw prints. In the spring, I watched the bark on the lilac close over the gashes. I have no idea to what world, if any, my friend, my father, Jeanne, had gone, whether any of them had sent the dog to me, whether the dog was somehow their spirits. What I do know is the dog and I acted out some silent drama that night. Neither of us said a thing. We moved together around a tree, and at the end of his tether, the world billowed outward and somehow I felt I was untangling my own griefs, knew that this silent, spiral-out ritual in the middle of a wide December night did more to help me let the dead go than did the memorial services, the poems of tribute, the nights of reminiscing. The dog appeared on a night when I'd felt emptied again by grief, and our movements, mundane as they were, took on the feel of ritual, became ecstatic, not in the joyful sense, but in the original sense of the word: *taken out of one's place, taken to a different place.* A larger place, a *shul*, in which a dog appeared.

You wait in the dark, in the blank absence, the void, and sooner or later, something appears, begins to take shape, something that could not have come into anything other than absence. Something, in fact, that needs absence first in order to have form later. In *Dream of the Underworld*, James Hillman says that "dimension sensed as loss is actually the presence of the void. . . . Here in depth there is space enough to take in the same physical world but in another way." A voice in the cave. A white dog.

Or stalactites. At Luray Caverns in Virginia, I entered underground rooms bejewelled in cave pearls and cave orchids, the exquisite white lace of aragonite, rooms lit up like palaces and hung with thousands of stalactites. The process begins in a limestone mountain reamed out by water. It begins with blank walls, a bare space in the dark. If it's a wet cave, then water drips into the emptiness, depositing calcite in tiny rings that grow after millions of years into all those fantastic shapes, all that dripping festoonery of stalactites and flowstone, thousands of burnished soda straws. In the midst of Luray's lit-up fantasia, it's hard to remember that spare beginning. But if you step off the path, peer into a side chasm where formations haven't grown, you won't forget you're underground in an ancient hole. You'll see only rough stone, uninterrupted blankness. Back on the main walkway, you'll see how all the now-decorated main caverns were, once, just slits in stone, how the walls inched back and back, how for thousands of years there was only an empty cave, full of dank air, the slow dripping of water.

Not even the splendor of the forms can obscure the original emptiness. I want to remember this, to see if I can pay attention to the lull between hollow and form. I have, in the act of writing, sensed the mind leaning across a blank space, reaching for story, artifice, something, anything, to complete the metaphor. I wonder if it's possible to pause that leap, to properly imagine that inscrutable space the mind leaps over. What kind of training or discipline would it take to linger for a few moments in that blank space, image-absent and unfilled? Could I see in slow motion how a drop of water dangles? Or how grief changes shape, lightens a little?

How hurt does too? A couple of years ago, I sat in a chair at the edge of the Thar Desert in India, not far from the Pakistani border. I'd been traveling with a lover who had just disclosed something that made me want to walk away, far away, out into the desert, to just keep walking across that flat, dry expanse. It was twilight. Someone brought us cups of chai, wanted to know if we wanted music. *No,* I said. I wanted nothing but the nothingness of the desert. I got up out of my chair, headed away from the small village, the dancers, the decorated camels, walked in the soft sand, the small grains working their way into my shoes. The desert drew me as surely as if it were a magnet and my body a collapsing stack of iron shavings. I kicked at anything, spat out a searing attack to the empty dunes. I wanted to pound something, his head, perhaps. The desert that evening stretched everywhere, its sands of gritty buff strangely lit beneath a high ceiling of lusterless dusk. I clomped one foot after another after another into the sand, which shifted just slightly. But nothing else happened. The wind didn't gust, the Pakistanis didn't come roaring over the border, I didn't feel fortified by the satisfaction of being the one so clearly wronged, and no one from the village came to bring me back. Nothing happened. When I turned around, I couldn't even see my tracks. Everything seemed swallowed up in the vastness, the endlessness of sand, that ancient Indian sky. And finally the need to lash out in revenge lessened. I didn't *have* to yell or sulk or grab the first flight home. It wasn't that the hurt lifted but that there was, out there in the desert, more room for hurt, and so it didn't press so hard. That familiar sense of needing to explode with emotion eased and it had to do, I think now, with not feeling so confined, so squeezed by, so dense with hurt. Plenty of room in a desert to feel what you feel, and plenty of time to decide what to do.

The next year I was back, farther north, where three friends and I traveled up the Ganges River, almost to its source, to find a Hindu holy man. At a ceremony the night before, a priest had pressed sandalwood into our foreheads, chanted, thrown sacred leaves into the river in the names of our children. Drums pounded, bells clanged, the village chanted. We took off our shoes, offered rupees and scarves, spent the night huddled in bed under blankets listening to the Ganges, and went groggily the next morning to the holy man's hut. I confess that I forget or didn't understand most of what he said. I do remember the lightheadedness at eleven thousand feet, the craggy Himalayas rising even higher around us, the cold, the noise of the river, glacial white, the tidiness of his tiny hut, his lively, piercing eyes, and a single image he offered in the midst of a rambling two-hour talk: The heart, he said softly, is the only real temple. Worship there. Everything else is distraction.

And weeks later, Sunithi, the elderly Indian woman to whom I'd told the desert story, said to me, "The heart, you know, is the widest secret space. That's where the spirit is free." She wrote *Guhaiya* in my notebook, the Sanskrit word for secret space. *Guhaiya*, which sounds like *Go here*. Everything else is distraction? I love India for its cow-jangling, horn-honking, sari-swaying excess, its lavish moon palaces and plumed elephants, the elaborate, erotic carvings on its temples. But the farther into any Indian temple you go, the less elaborate the carvings. The innermost sanctum is always dark and unadorned. Like the human spirit. *Guhaiya.*

The heart is a *shul?*

I don't wish to imply that a fleeting and delicate awareness of spaciousness is a gift of the Indian deserts, the Himalayas, a cave, or death. We stumble into our own hollowed-out interiors just by getting up and going to work every day, just by trying to stay reasonably alive. There are plenty of caverns inside our psyches, places that have been emptied by grief and losses we're not even aware of, plenty of stony pockets where water drips slowly and all the flashlight batteries are dead. Places, probably, where nothing happens, empty pathways, uninhabited tunnels. Here, too, are concealed worlds, the secret passageways, the dead-end chutes. Uninhabited space.

Not just in caves, temples, our own secret interiors, but all around us, too. It's the place that Rilke describes so beautifully:

> *Whoever you are: some evening take a step*
> *out of your house, which you know so well.*
> *Enormous space is near.*

In that enormous space, it's possible, he says, with the eye of imagination, to lift one tree, to raise it, to hold it up against the backdrop of sky, and "With that you have made the world." You crawl into a cavern, stand up in unexpected space, peer through a broken stalactite, imagine you can see the desert dunes. You walk outside into a winter night and there's a dog that will help unwind the tightness of grief. Is it possible that wide winter night, that enormous space, is everywhere around us? In the middle of Times Square, in a roomful of people? And *in* us? In all of *us,* somewhere, even in the cacophony of emotional confusion?

Guhaiya, Sunithi tells me. Secret space. *Go here,* she says, pointing to her chest. Wrapped in a brilliant orange sari, her wrists bangled with silver, a woman beautifully adorned, she's no ascetic. She isn't advocating renunciation; she's trying to tell me that space is ether, the element that's greater than all other elements, greater than earth, fire, water, wind; that it is space which permeates all other matter. It's *here,* where the small circumference of our lives moves outward, and what's possible has nothing to do with solace or salvation or redemption, but something more important: the possibility of opening to an intimacy with a larger world.

Go inside a stone, Charles Simic says. Who knows what's in there? The fantasia of myriad dripping stones, cave orchids, rimstone pools. A voice. An unexpected openheartedness, generosity. A white dog. Maybe a moon, Simic muses, some reflected light, strange writings and maps: *star-charts on the inner walls.*

I remember once standing outside a cave in the Southwest desert. Before the bats come out from it in the evening, they swarm underground, thousands of them, flying sometimes for half a mile below the surface before emerging up and out of the entrance. It looks as if the cave's dark interior has peeled off its walls, is rising from belowground up into the wide pre-night, scattering in circles and whirls, flinders of cave black-glittering the sky. I have felt my heart race there, my stomach flutter, thousands of small wings beating inside. I've watched the way a graceful swoop shatters into erratic drop and veer. I've felt grief do the same.

The bats feed all night, devouring mosquitoes, snagging gnats in midair. The sky is full of flapping hands. Before dawn they turn back. From a hundred feet up, they find in the dark the darker fold in the earth that means cave. They swoop down and enter it. They fold their wing-hands, they're home, inside, where there's plenty of room for thousands of tiny hearts.

First emptiness, then form. Probably emptiness again. It's the sequence I want to keep in mind, the undulating wave of something rising out of nothing, dissolving again, the practice of paying attention to the lull. The viscera of absence call us to grope where we can't see, where the normal constraints, the habits, identities, and the definitions by which we live might lift, disperse momentarily, leave us in enormous space. Here the imagination twists and searches, fumbles, gets ready to say what we can't quite see. We stand in the absence, in the clearing, the hollowed-out place and discover, not wisdom or enlightenment, but spaciousness. Room. A *shul*.